WHAT WERE THEY <u>THINKING?</u>

(2nd Edition)

WHAT WERE THEY THINKING?

Inside the Minds of Trump's Voters

by

Evelyn Roberts Brooks

ISBN:

978-1-7322080-0-1 (ebook)
978-1-7322080-1-8 (paperback)

What Were They Thinking: Inside the Minds of Trump's Voters/
Evelyn Roberts Brooks – 2nd Ed.

Categories:

Nonfiction > Political Humor
Humor & Entertainment > Humor > Political

Photo credits:

This book is intended to provide information and is not meant to prescribe, diagnose, treat, offer medical, psychological, or other professional advice. The author encourages you to explore this book if the material is of interest to you. You accept full responsibility for your own actions and choices. The author disclaims responsibility for what you might or might not do with the teachings or information in this book. Please use the information responsibly.

Evelyn explains the laws of the mind in her big fat juicy book *YOU WERE BORN TO TRIUMPH: Create a Five-Star Life in Your Quantum Kitchen*

To learn more about Evelyn and read her hundreds of informational articles and blog posts about spiritual healing, stress relief, and using the laws of the mind, do a Google search for: "Evelyn Roberts Brooks" … or simply go to her central website evelynbrooks.com

Would you like to learn how to dissolve guilt, reduce your stress, and stop letting regrets for the past and worry about the future tie your stomach in knots? Stop by today to claim free Instant Download Access to a powerful Serenity Gift Collection at evelynbrooks.com

Find Evelyn's books at:
booksbyevelyn.com

Follow Evelyn at:
twitter.com/evelynbrooks
facebook.com/evelynbrooksauthor
youtube.com/evelynbrooks
pinterest.com/evelynRbrooks

View and share the #FreedomFighters book and videos:
FreedomFightersBook.com
FreedomFightersVideos.com

Books by Evelyn Roberts Brooks

Keep up to date by visiting booksbyevelyn.com

When you finish the book, please take a moment to review it (and give me a 4- or 5-star rating if you'd like) so other readers can find me, too. I really appreciate it. I love hearing from readers—contact me at evelynbrooks.com

or

my Facebook EvelynBrooksAuthor page

<u>Liberty and Justice Series</u>

AMERICA'S NEW BREED OF FREEDOM FIGHTERS: With Liberty and Justice for All

WHAT WERE THEY THINKING? Inside the Minds of Trump's Voters <u>[Political humor]</u>

WHAT TRUMP'S VOTERS WERE REALLY THINKING: The Complete Report Unedited <u>[Political</u>

humor]

WHEN THEY GO LOW WE GO HIGH: Tending Our Garden of Democracy

RESTORING TIBET: Global Action Plan to Send the Dalai Lama Home

Born to Triumph Series

YOU WERE BORN TO TRIUMPH: Create a Five-Star Life in Your Quantum Kitchen

FIVE PROVEN METHODS TO STOP SELF-SABOTAGE

DO'S AND DON'TS FOR RECOVERING PEOPLE-PLEASERS

SIX SECRETS FOR A NO-FAULT MARRIAGE

CALLING ALL LIGHTWORKERS

CHOOSE HAPPINESS NOW

HEAL YOUR TOXIC FRIENDSHIPS

YOUR GRIEF RELIEF: Heal the Void

FORGET YOUR TROUBLES: Enjoy Your Life Today

GET HAPPY TODAY: No More Excuses!

BE HEALTHY, BE RICH: Secrets of Wellness and Wealth (classics by Wallace D. Wattles, annotated)

Fiction: Adult and Young Adult

THE DREAM SPINNERS (a novel about love, loss, and second chances with a little help from the Other Side)

THE GYPSY TALISMAN

THE CALICO TAPESTRY

VAMPIRE MISCHIEF

Juvenile Fiction

PROFESSOR BUBBLES AND THE MISSING FORMULA: A Law of Attraction Mystery for Middle Graders

"Somewhere I have read that every end
is a new beginning. At this moment I am at a corner.
If there is a beginning on the other side of it,
I cannot see what it is."

Patricia Wentworth

"Two percent of the people think;
three percent of the people think they think;
and ninety-five percent of the people
would rather die than think."

George Bernard Shaw

"A merry heart doeth good
like a medicine:
but a broken spirit drieth the bones."

Proverbs 17:22

"A day without laughter is a day wasted."

Charlie Chaplin

"The present President [Trump],
in the very beginning he mentioned
'America first.' That sounded in
my ear not very nice."

His Holiness the 14th Dalai Lama

Dedication

To the comedians
who uplift our morale
in times of fear and darkness
and help us find the courage
to keep moving forward.

Contents

Preface to the 2nd Edition

Dear Reader,

What's the point of laughter? Seriously, why do we laugh at Charlie Chaplin's pratfalls, at a dog spinning in circles trying to catch its own wagging tail, at a toddler trying to pull a fistful of cookies out of a narrow-mouthed cookie jar?

We laugh because it is part of the human experience of joy.

We laugh because it gives us relief from our woes.

We laugh because a hearty belly-laugh produces happy hormones that flood our body with a sense of wellbeing.

But what happens inside when what we are laughing at is the antics of a Republican president and his cabinet and congressional leaders who are pillaging and looting the wealthiest country in the world for their own benefit, and to repay the big corporations who funded their campaigns?

That kind of laughter can leave a sour residue. We may walk away from the comedy routine feeling even worse about ourselves and the state of the union. We might also come away feeling "superior" to Trump's voters, but that's not a healthy situation for any of us.

Let's create a framework for compassion and understanding to thrive. I believe that everyone wants to be happy, to have opportunities to grow and prosper. Donald Trump has proven to be a tremendous catalyst for progressives around the world to rise up and become active in the political scene. And that's a good thing.

When we focus on alleviating the suffering of others in our country--those who are affected the most by Republican Party actions such as tax cuts for the super-wealthy, reduction in health care and social programs that help the middle class and lower income families —then we can transform our own worry and fear into positive, progressive action.

My aim in writing this book is to not only provide some relief with humor, but to reveal the inner workings of a paradigm (mindset; a collection of beliefs) that not only elected Donald Trump in November 2016, but keeps his fans blind to the truth about his actions.

> *To a man with few scruples,*
> *the moral opposition he expected*
> *might have seemed a temporary*
> *dislodgeable obstinacy,*
> *not an immovably embedded barrier.*
> **-- Dick Francis**

Please read the quote above from one of my favorite novelists, Dick Francis, in which the hero is speaking of the fictional villain in "Bolt." I found the description appropriate for a book about Donald Trump, so, therefore, allow me to officially welcome you as a valuable member of the "Immovably Embedded Barrier" aka The Resistance.

It seems that at this point in history, Republican voters are more deeply compelled to protect their paradigm than ever before, no matter what their party leaders do and how far those actions may be from their own core values. The Republican voter paradigm is the belief system that tells them their party leaders act in the best interests of the American people, and that anything Democrats say to the contrary is simply a pack of lies.

Denial is always the easy way out. It allows us to keep on pretending that things will magically get better and that we have nothing to do with the results we are experiencing. Ask any addict: it's terrifying to look at your own behavior and admit that no one forced you into this hole.

For Republican voters today, it probably feels too scary to take a look at the facts. Continuing to support Trump is much easier on the nerves than admitting that you've backed the wrong party.

When I thought of creating this second edition of *What Were They Thinking?*, I planned to include a new section that would catalog at least the top twenty of the horrible things Donald Trump and his buddies in Congress not only planned but began enacting since his election, as well as a summary of the deplorable State of the Union with the Republicans in charge.

But then...I realized how depressing that research would be. And when you began reading the list, our collective strength would falter, because we would feel upset instead of empowered; we'd feel outraged instead of inspired; we'd feel despair instead of hope.

If you're a Democrat or Progressive, you already know what you'll find.

If you're still a Trump Supporter, you won't believe anything against him no matter what I say.

We all know what happens when someone tries to "convince" us that they are right and we are wrong: we simply dig in our heels and hold tight to our position as if our very life depends on it.

But... humor can sneak past our paradigm and open windows for us to see a broader perspective than the one we are clinging to.

Laughter opens the door to change.

Look at the facts. And then let's turn our attention toward undoing the damage, healing and moving forward with love in our hearts for all citizens of this world.

Instead of focusing on what "they" are doing to destroy our nation, let's keep our energy on what "we" can do to protect it and heal our country.

Let's lighten up and free our innate power to create progress and change. Laughter is the way to release our tension so we can work more effectively in support of liberty and justice for all and not just for a few.

Too often, political humor is intended only to throw barbs at the opposition. Let's remind ourselves to shine the spotlight on our own part in the political environment that allowed a man like Donald Trump to be elected. His rants and wild promises appealed to millions of people who are angry about life and feel threatened by diversity and progress.

We can and should lighten the fears and worries of others around us, including our Republican neighbors.

I hope this book will be a source of positive and energizing relief for Democrats, Progressives and Liberals. My goal is to help lighten your spirit in the face of the destruction and violations of human rights created by the Republican Party and its leaders, and to help create a shift in our collective consciousness so that we can move forward.

When we laugh, we can open our minds to create positive change in the world. But no one can pry our minds open for us, we must do it ourselves by being willing to broaden our perspective and uplift our actions.

In this second edition of *What Were They Thinking?: Inside the Minds of Trump's Voters*, you will find a new essay titled **"The Restorative Power of Laughter"** along with the entire first edition of the book.

I hope you enjoy this new edition and, again, welcome to The Resistance.

Blessings,

Evelyn

Evelyn Roberts Brooks

P.S. I hope you enjoy my tribute to humorist Erma Bombeck in the final chapter. I like to think she'd endorse this book.

The Restorative Power of Laughter

Laughter helps us release anger, freeing us to create more good in the world. When we live at a higher and more loving level, we can respond to troubling situations and shine the light of compassion and progress on them. We can create healing.

Anger is a powerful emotion. Perhaps you were raised the way I was, to believe that nice people don't get angry.

As part of the Good Girl Syndrome, we're taught that anger is a bad thing, and you are naughty if you feel it. So we stuff it down, but it doesn't go away. We learn to smile without meaning it, while seething inside about what others are doing. We compound our upset feelings with guilt and shame that we feel these "bad" emotions.

Without healing, the anger festers into resentment and bitterness, and then it crops up in physical manifestations such as rashes, headaches, high blood pressure and even cancer.

So let's deal with anger about Donald Trump and his SS (Syncopated Sociopaths*) in a healthy way. We want to release the rage—because anger keeps us in magnetic alignment with a low-level awareness of life.

*"In music, syncopation involves a variety of rhythms which are in some way unexpected, which make part or all of a tune or piece of music off-beat." (courtesy of Wikipedia)

*"Sociopaths are people who have little to no conscience. They will lie, cheat, steal and manipulate others for their own benefit. They know exactly what they are doing; they just don't care because they don't think that way." (courtesy of Urban Dictionary)

A Russian writer named Maxim Gorky, who lived in the late 19th to early 20th century, wrote: "All of us are pilgrims on this earth. I have even heard people say that the Earth itself is a pilgrim in the heavens."

A pilgrim may be seen as someone who goes on a journey—a traveler or wanderer, especially in a foreign land—in other words, where things are unfamiliar. You're surrounded by strangers rather than people and events that are familiar and customary to you.

In today's political climate in America, many millions of us feel that we are walking in an alien land where those in charge glibly enact new laws of destruction and mayhem, where civil liberties are curtailed, and basic health care and education are threatened on a daily basis.

And yet you look around and see that those very leaders are lauded and applauded by millions of your fellow citizens. It seems like you landed in the Twilight Zone. And it doesn't seem there is anything to laugh about.

Let me invite you to be a pilgrim in your own life. Be someone who is a tip of the arrow thinker, a pilgrim moving ahead into growth and transformation.

Most people lead a reactive life because we're trained to live that way—to react to our conditions, circumstances, everything that's going on around us and in the news.

Most of us stay in the victim level of awareness our entire life. It's what we see modeled around us and unless we learn a better way, we keep on reacting to what goes on.

However, as we develop our mental awareness to a higher level, we learn to respond to conditions, rather than letting conditions control us.

In the position of this calmer awareness, we can observe the behavior of others, and then determine our course of action. Even when we are mocked and derided by those who are still trapped in a paradigm of fear, we can keep moving forward.

With the power of laughter, we can avoid being pulled down into despair. We can maintain a humorous outlook at the foibles of humanity...while we continue working for liberty and justice, and for the basic freedoms that all men and women of the world deserve to enjoy: food, clothing, shelter, transportation, health care, freedom of worship, freedom of personal relationship choices, freedom from oppression, opportunities to do meaningful and satisfying work in service of others.

Humor can lead the way to enlightenment.

Introduction

Presidents Day 2017

Dear Reader,

This book is my love song to America. I hope that it provides a respite for marchers and protestors, balm for the weary soul, inspiration to ignite hope for the future, and the relaxing warmth of shared laughter for the heart clenched in fear.

Although it started as a different kind of book, it turned out that I wanted to talk to you about thinking and about what happens when we are lazy with our thinking habits. But I wanted to do it in a way that would bring relief, instead of more tension over serious topics that have so many people heartsore and weary.

I got the idea for my second book about the 2016 election while crossing Fifth Avenue to Central Park last Saturday with my dog Sugar Bear. I was thinking about Trump's voters and musing: *But what were they THINKING?!*

Realizing it was a great idea for a book, I felt that if I could quickly put it together and release it on Presidents Day, it would be a fitting follow-up for *America's New Breed of Freedom Fighters* which came out on Inauguration Day.

Initially my idea was simply a humorous book for Hillary supporters, and all the protestors and marchers combatting Trump's agenda. The title would be "What Trump's Voters Were REALLY Thinking" and the interior would be completely blank: 150 pages without even a message or explanation from me. The idea was done effectively by Dr. Alan Francis with his book "Everything Men Know About Women" in 1983, during the birth of self-help sections at bookstores, and I thought it could be applied to the Trump Issue to great effect.

As a writer, I take my craft seriously. I understand the power of words to soothe or inflame, to mollify or irritate, to harm or to heal.

Whoever coined the phrase "Sticks and stones can break my bones but words will never hurt me" was a sadist, an ignoramus, or a bullying victim desperate to find relief by grasping at straws.

I suspect it was the victim, as I was frequently bullied in childhood and went on into relationships with men who also bullied me. I know what it's like to feel desperate for a glimmer of hope to cling to, that something will magically change. Perhaps it's the deep reason I am so outraged that people who should know better voted for Donald Trump, Bully Extraordinaire.

Our words are powerful, far more powerful than we've been taught.

I decided it would be more useful to serve up some humor along with a series of voter "surveys," essays, skits, movie quotes, and other content that would support progressive ideals and stimulate ideas about creating more growth and expansion, more liberty and justice in our nation. The "fake" book is also included at the end of this one, as a Bonus—it's not entirely empty, so take a look at my comments in it.

Together, we stand strong and we will not surrender to the Trump Administration's clear intention of destroying essential freedoms across our land.

This is a time of great potential to show what we believe in.

About 24% of the eligible voters in America voted for Donald Trump. That's nothing close to a "majority." Let's not forget that.

We aren't battling "half the nation" – we are battling apathy and disinterest, people who feel their vote doesn't make a difference, who are stuck in a low level of interest or awareness about the power of a president to create war and devastation upon a whim. We are battling the minds of average Republicans who see only what they want to see, and filter everything through their mindset of "might makes right" and "my Party right or wrong."

I have deliberately assigned this book to the category of

"humor"—because I hope it will lighten the nation's mood and give encouragement to protestors, and also because a label of "humor" places the book in that nebulous land somewhere between nonfiction and fiction which allows me more creative freedom to say what I want to say, even with the use of imaginary surveys and polls, dreams and fables.

Realizing I had barely a week to write and publish this book, I allowed myself to daydream about collaborating with a writing team. We'd sit around a big table, toss out ideas, shape and expand them and leaven them with the higher vibration of laughter to uplift the audience of readers we kept in mind at all times ... and as I started to sigh wistfully, and turn back to my solitary task, I remembered: *We are all connected in the One Mind.*

So, I called on some of my favorite comedy writers and comedians who are no longer with us in 3D Technicolor and Surround Sound, but are certainly still with us in spirit: Billy Wilder, Robin Williams, Harold Ramis, John Belushi, Gene Wilder, John Ritter, Gilda Radner, Madeline Kahn, Dom DeLuise, Harvey Corman, Tim Conway, Lucille Ball, Mary Tyler Moore, Cleavon Little, Phil Hartman, and anyone else available from the Comedy Hall of Fame.

I dubbed these valiant friends my "Invisible Comedy Writing Team" because when I pleaded for help in writing this book, they generously contributed far beyond my expectations, with one idea after another. Any scenes or chapters that go over like a lead balloon are entirely due to my own tendency

14

to expound on a topic and get too intense. The buck stops here.

Before we begin, let me remind you about the powerful law of attraction that is in action every moment of the day 24/7, and the basic steps to manifestation: Hold the thought. Feel it. Believe it. Imagine it is already true. Take inspired action in that direction. It must manifest.

We used the same process to inadvertently elect Donald but we didn't wield our power correctly. Without realizing it, we acted more like Mickey Mouse waving the sorcerer's wand, unaware that we were creating results in every direction we pointed. So now we can step out of a cartoon and look to the other Pluto (the planet instead of Mickey's dog) and the wonder of our universe. Let the sun and the stars remind us that the world is still turning and each day brings new opportunities to create either more fear in the world and all its attendant ills, or more good and the joy that comes with growth.

Trump is not mentally fit to be the President of the United States. This is not news to Democrats, but apparently even Republicans are beginning to recognize his behavior should not be allowed to continue.

Humor doesn't have to mean sarcasm or putting others down or belittling people. I hope I have not been guilty of sarcasm or undue cruelty in this book—my aim was to shine a bright light on areas that need help, and inspire you to keep

15

marching forward on the road of progress.

I'll be right there alongside you.

with love,

Evelyn

Evelyn Roberts Brooks

P.S. For free ebooks, access to my studio with webinars, coaching lessons, and other downloadable material related to being a Freedom Fighter, visit your gift page at evelynbrooks.com/readers-freedom-fighters

Chapter 1

The Power of "What If?"

Every story in life begins with these magical words: *What if...?*

What if we met two down-on-their-luck musicians in 1920s Chicago, and what if they witnessed a mob shooting, and what if the gangsters found out who they were, and what if the only way out of town was to dress like women and join an all-girl band headed to Florida, and then what if just when they thought they were safe, the gangsters came to Florida for a mobsters' convention, and what if...?

The result of all those "what ifs" and more: *Some Like it Hot* (1959) written by Billy Wilder and I.A.L. Diamond.

What if there was this spoiled belle named Scarlett in 1860s Atlanta who met a dashing guy named Rhett, and what if they fell in love and what if, when he pointed out that she was being selfish, she had an ah-ha moment, changed her ways, and happily sewed clothes out of her draperies for the poor children, and then what if they got married and never shared a quarrelsome word again...?

Nope. That version of *Gone with the Wind* wouldn't keep our interest, would it?

We humans are seemingly hard-wired for conflict and drama, as well as the Hero's Journey.

No Hero's Journey opens with something bad happening and the likeable boy-next-door dashes off to save the day, then returns and his life goes back to normal.

We wouldn't tolerate that kind of bad writing. We know that in the true Hero's Journey, when there is a threat and our likeable guy is called on to help, he <u>refuses</u>! He's no dummy: he knows it's a dangerous mission. He points out all the reasons he's not qualified, he can't leave home at this time, pick somebody else. Then something else happens that worsens the situation, something like Donald Trump's getting elected. And suddenly that everyday kind of person who was minding his/her own business is thrust into a turning point in Life: retreat and hope somebody else will fix everything OR join the resistance, work for change, and together transform the evil situation so Goodness can prevail.

In that same Hero's Journey there is always a "What if" which the writer carefully crafts in response to the story outline that calls for your heart to drop and your breath to catch: *All Is Lost!*

This is the part of our story—and we are all in this chapter of human history together, so let's call it a "story" – where it seems like nothing we do matters, or it seems like the evil forces are far too strong for our capabilities.

Understand that in every hero's journey this is simply a plot point, a necessary time to gather our strength and push up and out of a lower level of existence and onto a higher plane. It's growth, it's expansion, it's part of humanity's evolvement. And we are in the very thick of it! What a great time to be alive—to know we can make a huge difference for future generations by what we commit to today.

This is the low point in the story where it seems there is no chance to defeat the monster, the villain, the zombies, the raging fire, or the enemy you've been sleeping with.

But then, our hero digs deep within, and taps into that bottomless well of strength we all possess whether we know it or not. He looks to his companions for assistance, because we never have to fight alone, and then he finds a new way to approach the situation, thus leading us to the climax where – in a Hero's Journey and also in a comedy – the hero prevails and we get a Happy Ending.

In tragedies, the hero is defeated, and life is gloomy, dark – the type of ending you'll find in the genre of *film noir*, such as *Double Indemnity* (1944) written by Billy Wilder and Raymond Chandler, based on the novel by James M. Cain.

It's up to us now. How will we use the power of our collective "What if…" to create the change we desire?

Will we create a tragedy that goes on year after year by saying and picturing:

What if Trump gets away with everything he has planned?

What if Trump builds the wall, starts a war, deports everyone he hates (hey, that means we're all vulnerable because narcissists have no loyalty even to their henchmen), starts a recession/depression/market crash/housing crash...

What if Trump gets re-elected?

OR

Will we create a miracle?

Will this crisis bring more and more people in increasing numbers into a greater awareness that they really do count and they really can make a difference by stepping up and joining the protestors and contacting their elected representatives and signing petitions and talking to nonvoters?

Will we gain a better understanding of the laws of the mind and how we can combine our Thinking Power with our What If Power and change things around, blast up and out of the low point of "All Is Lost" and into a brighter future by envisioning a much more beneficial outcome for America and our allies around the world?

Will we continue to support journalists who report what is going on and who refuse to tell the lies Trump and his team demand (such as how many people were in those white tents on Inauguration Day)?

Will we continue to hold Trump accountable in the press, in social media, and in our protest marches?

Will we teach our children that just because a man like that managed to be elected President of the United States doesn't mean we should emulate his so-called core values?

I believe Democrats, Progressive, and enlightened Republicans will continue to say: *What if I can make a difference by speaking up?*

Let's do it.

Chapter 2

Survey of TVs (Trump Voters)

This book actually contains the results of two "surveys" of Trump voters. The second one can be found at Chapter 12 Vulcan Mind-Meld with Trump's Voters.

This chapter shares the responses in my first questionnaire, which focused solely on asking his supporters…

"WHY Did You Vote for Donald Trump?"

My first survey launched on November 9, 2016—yes, the day after the election I got busy mailing out survey questionnaires to 60-odd million Republican voters across America.

Odd:

1. Not an even number;
2. A rounded-off number, or estimate;
3. Strange, peculiar; an out of the ordinary occurrence;
4. Puzzling, inexplicable, unbelievable.

This survey was in the nature of an exit poll, but on a much grander scale. Even though there was only one question in the survey, respondents had a full page to write their reply, and I enclosed a prepaid return envelope for their convenience.

Out of 60 million letters mailed, I got only 133 replies.

I'm not sure if that low interest rate is a response in itself, but let's soldier on and look at the results together.

Perhaps they were embarrassed to take the survey, even though total anonymity was assured. In fact, you will not find a single name in this survey report, nor any other identifying information that might reveal who these voters are in their everyday lives, nor where they live. Although the survey sample is rather small, I believe it is representative of the general Trump tribe and why they chose him.

How did I fund such a massive undertaking? I didn't do it alone. My trusty companion, Sugar Bear, volunteered her services. She is a cream colored Golden retriever and so sweet and gentle that even people who don't like dogs come up and ask if they can pet her. It gets so I have to wash her head after a walk in Central Park because, frankly, some people don't mind patting her when they have sticky fingers or have just cleaned up after their own dog. (*I know: eeeuw!*)

Sugar Bear offered virtual hugs to Democrats, and the money began pouring in. With nearly 66 million Hillary voters (plus their children and dogs) sending anywhere from $1 to $100 just to get a Skype smile from my dog, you can imagine how quickly the funds piled up.

Go ahead, I'll let you do the math. All right, if you're math challenged, imagine the average was just $20. Now multiply that by 65,844,610. Wait, make that 65,844,609 because I took my own name off the list. I get hugs from Sugar Bear at no charge every day.

Yes indeed, my dog earned 10 figures in a matter of days, amounting to about 1.5 billion US dollars. I bought her a new collar with her name spelled out on it in cubic zirconia stones.

Of course there were expenses: printing, envelopes, postage, helpers to prepare the mailings. (Work at home! Earn $$$ stuffing envelopes!)

I felt that a special touch for mail to Republicans was buying sheet after sheet of Rosa Parks commemorative stamps from the post office so I had plenty on hand to stamp each letter.

In case you don't recall who she was, Ms. Parks was an African-American who refused to give up her seat on a bus in Montgomery, Alabama back in the days when "people of color" were supposed to sit in the back (or risk bullying, both verbal and physical, as well as arrest). Her strength and determination and quiet defiance led to a boycott of that bus system and helped people see the ugly truth about segregation laws. Her actions helped bring Martin Luther King, Jr. into the nation's spotlight. As an early activist for Civil Rights in the 1960s, Parks is an important part of American history.

Someone asked me the other day if I declared all that money -- 1.5 billion dollars! -- on my 2016 income tax return. I laughed. After all, if President Trump doesn't have to pay income tax, why should I?

If anyone demands to see my tax return, I'll just take a page out of his admittedly small book and say, "My return is being audited and I can't release it until that audit is over." It won't matter how many times you point out, as Hillary and the debate moderator did, that Trump could have released his return at any time, audit or not. He hid behind a rehearsed comment and I'll do the same. I'll just be a broken record and say I can't release it until my lawyer says it's okay.

Pretty nifty trick, isn't it? Just ignore those pesky laws, and get elected President!

SURVEY RESULTS: Some respondents made similar comments, so they were tabulated together. Following are the statements received in reply to my exit poll survey:

*My family always votes Republican, so I did, too.

*Fox News told me how awful that Hillary is!

*I've seen Trump on The Apprentice and he's got a lot of money, so he'll be good for the economy.

*My great-granddaddy voted against Votes for Women, my daddy voted against the Equal Rights Amendment, and there was no way in hell I was gonna vote for a woman president.

*We need jobs in my town and Trump promised to bring manufacturing work back from China. Fox News said to trust him.

*Melania would make a really cool First Lady—love yur clothes, girl!

*I'm a white man, and I'm sick and tired of all these other guys and gals getting preferential treatment time and again. I'm done! I've had it! I'm mad as hell and I'm not going to take it anymore! Besides, everybody knows he's secretly a Nazi and I remember my history classes—that guy Hitler got things done.

*America is for white Christians, and I know I can count on Trump to make us great again.

*I'm mad as hell and so is Donald and so that must mean he's my kinda guy!

*I'm for the 2nd Amendment.

*I don't want another career politician or one of these Constitutional lawyers. Eggheads! Let's give somebody else a shot at running the country!

*Get rid of the bleeding heart liberals and this country could go back to what it's supposed to be like.

*Drill, baby, drill. It's there for the taking, so we should take it.

*Build the damn wall and keep out people who don't look like me or go to my kind of church.

*Get rid of people who look different.

*The Democrats are lying when they say Trump is against (pick one or more): a decent minimum wage; health care for all; affordable education; human rights; women's reproductive rights and access to cancer screening; Social Security and Medicare. [This was a popular reply, so I combined the separate responses into one.]

*Climate change is just one of those catchwords to make us buy something we don't need or put restrictions on air quality and shit like that what we can do—ridiculous!

*I liked Reagan. Let's give Trump a chance. I think they're the same height, aren't they?

*Even the liberal reporters kowtowed to Trump, so I knew all that other stuff Hillary kept spouting about Trump not being qualified was just the Democrats jealous because he's got so much money, probably more money than God.

*I mean, like, with all that money, who wouldn't want him to be President?

*It means we'll get more jobs from all his companies and stuff like that. I'd like that.

*Well, he's got more than one big building with his name on top and his name all over the front of the building and probably his name is on the toilet paper in the lobby restroom, and everybody gets out of his way when he goes by—does Hillary have anything even close to that?

*Let's face the fact everyone is secretly thinking: We'll all be better off with a white guy back in the White House and get things back to normal.

*Trump is going to be better for the economy! He says it over and over and so I believe him.

*I can count on Trump to get rid of laws I don't like and never did—like all that Civil Rights crap that was shoved down our throats in the 60s and 70s.

*He'll make America great for Americans, not all those people from other countries coming in here to take over. I say lock the door and keep 'em out, now that me and my family are here.

*Real Americans don't have names like Bautista and Kumar and Abdalla. Jones and Smith and Johnson are good enough for America. So is Trump.

*Trump says he never pays income tax because he doesn't have to—I want to find out how to do that, too!

*If God wanted a woman in the White House, then why wasn't Martha Washington our first President? Duh.

*I'm tired of being out of work and Trump promised jobs. I heard him say it on the TV so it must be true.

*I'm military. Whole family is, and a lot of my friends, too. I heard some crap about veterans and even some of my buddies on active duty saying Trump is a Blue Falcon, not somebody you'd trust to have your back, but I bet Hillary paid them to say it. I mean, military and Republicans just kind of go together, don't they?

*My ex was named Hillary. No way was I going down that path again.

*I'm not saying I like everything he talks about, but most of that is just campaign chat to get attention in the news, and he won't really do all that stuff when he's elected. He's just playing the game, a natural politician.

*He put millions of his own dollars in his own campaign— you just got to respect a man who believes in himself that much. That's integrity.

*Hello? Why do people keep chanting about "rights"— haven't they heard of the Bill of Rights? We've already got all the rights we need. It's just stupid. Now can I get back to my game?

*Everybody I know votes Republican. Is there some reason I shouldn't?

*Everything people said about Trump that was bad is just a bunch of lies. (Fox News told me so, and so did my pastor.)

*Jesus told me in a dream that when he talked about "Love

thy neighbor as thyself," he meant people who look like me and go to my church, not those other people, the ones who are so pushy about rights this and rights that. I love my neighbors. I do.

*This is anonymous, right? Cuz my wife would kill me if she finds out I said this but, okay, so it'll be a real relief to have that black man out of the White House and there's no way I was gonna put a woman in his place!

*What threat? Democrats are always so dramatic, saying things are falling apart. My life is just fine, thank you very much.

*He said he will help blue collar guys get jobs. My pastor said to trust that he will.

*Oh, spare me another intellectual debate. Yada, yada, yada. Like Trump says, if you don't like what someone is saying, just bomb 'em!

One respondent mailed back the questionnaire but he didn't answer the question. Instead he scrawled on the response form, in red crayon: "Your a joke! Your just trying to make money off Republicans with your stupid survey! Go hug a tree or something, you idiot libberal!"

I sent him back a polite, handwritten note: Thank you for taking the time to reply to my survey. However, if you are going to tell me that I am a "joke," in the future please use proper grammar. "You're" is the correct way to contract the words "you" and "are," not "your." And you misspelled "liberal."

I didn't bother to point out that I was not making money on the free survey, and in fact it had cost me more than my dog earned so that I was dipping into my own pocket to buy stamps: I have found that logic is not a strong suit for most Trump voters.

Chapter 3

Trump Exposed

I want to take a moment to publicly applaud the protestors in Red States where they are outnumbered but they still speak up and speak out on the issues dear to them and to our country's true progress. It's one thing to join a massive crowd in Washington, D.C. or New York City and other metropolitan areas, but I imagine it must be a daunting challenge when the group is smaller and the "opposition" know where you live and work.

It's also easier to chat with friends, to discuss our views when we're in the safety of a circle of friends and family who think the same way, and again takes more gumption to go outside your own door, to march and protest when your neighbors are Trump supporters. Thank you all, for not backing down.

Mr. Trump has made it abundantly clear he wants to gag free speech, and Republicans seem to think that's a great idea! No more free speech, unless you are praising Donald Trump, of course. Then you can say all you want.

Several Republican politicians in Red States have actually

initiated legislative bills to make it legal to arrest protestors for no reason other than the fact they are protesting Trump, to run down protestors with your car, again only for the reason the people holding signs are against Trump's administration. (By the way, I sure do wish I was making this up to get a laugh, but reports of these bills and more are scarily true.)

So, if you're feeling nervous about marching and protesting even though you really do want to join in the resistance, just do what public speakers are taught to do when they are nervous: Imagine your audience is only dressed in their underwear.

It's supposed to be a technique to level the playing field so that you don't feel "they" are superior to you.

We are all alike! Yea! We all wear underwear! (Well, at least most people do, I think…er, hope.)

So let's take a look at Mr. Trump without those expensive shirts, suits and ties. Now, I'm not saying there's anything wrong with wearing clothes that aren't from Macy's basement sale, but it can be intimidating if you see the outer-wear and judge someone's worth on the basis of that.

If you decide to deride or admire, base it on the person's speech and actions, not on what they wear.

Okay, I've got my special glasses on—borrowed from Superman—this is a really cool pair of specs because it's not

X-ray vision – who cares about Trump's bones and how many nickels he swallowed as a kid thinking that was the way to make money grow?

These glasses peel off the outer layer of clothing and let you see the undergarments below.

So let's take a quick peek. I'm not much of a voyeur but since I'm the writer of this book, I'll be brave and go first.

Wow, I have to admit that I'm surprised at what I see. The suit, the shirt, the tie—gone! And there's Donald Trump in an ordinary Hanes undershirt with a V-neck, and boxer shorts.

Wait. It's not Hanes. The shirt's label is sticking up and I see it was made in China. Hope he doesn't like Hanes—they finally exported their work from the USA to El Salvador for cheaper labor, but they don't use China—and once Trump's fancy-dancy wall against Mexico and Central America goes up, well, there goes his chance of getting a nice soft Hanes undershirt.

Hey, the price tag is hanging from the t-shirt's sleeve. I didn't know they made $1,000 undershirts. Maybe China is growing Egyptian cotton now?

Who leaves a price tag on their underwear? It's crinkly and fading, clearly having been through the wash a few times. Maybe the tag serves as a reminder about being superior to everyone else because you can afford to pay way more than average for your clothes?

I've seen more than enough with the view of his undershirt, but I want to give you a complete report and not shirk my duty. So here goes. I take in a deep breath and glance at the boxer shorts.

OMG! I've never seen a gold monogram and a crown on boxer shorts. (I'm just grateful he doesn't wear a thong, because I might be forced to take a gander at the rear view.)

There's something written in embroidery thread beneath the crown. I can't quite make out what it says. It doesn't appear to be in English. Could it be a foreign phrase? Hmm, doesn't look like Russian.

I activate the zoom feature on Superman's glasses and realize at once that the text is indeed English, but it was embroidered backwards for some odd reason.

Why would anyone...? Oh, I get it. It's written in reverse – so he can read it in the mirror while brushing his teeth. The phrase says:

!nɒm ɒ6 ɒo|Ꙅ

Do you suppose he realizes the probable origin of the slang

expression "You da man!" is Urban Black?

As far as imagining others in their underwear goes, it seems kind of distracting to me. How far do you carry this imagery? Are the guys suddenly Calvin Klein models and all the women are Victoria's Secret Angels even though they are wearing sweats or jeans and clingy knit tops that bulge where bulges weren't intended by Mother Nature? What about those images of granny pants and mesh briefs and slips with a strap held together by a safety pin. Does anyone even wear slips anymore?

Or are we more interested in that slip of the tongue when someone reveals his inner thoughts?

Now let's turn to Steve Bannon and see if we can't humanize him by noticing what kind of underwear the puppet master wears.

On the other hand…

Let's not, and say we did.

Chapter 4

This Mess Calls for a Giant Pooper Scooper

Show me a Trump supporter who actually explored the issues before voting (and didn't run away screaming), and I'll show you my pet dragon.

The first rule for writers is: write what you know about. That means I write primarily about creating a happier life while developing your potential to a higher level. I write screenplays (rom-com and family comedy). I also know more than a little about the laws of the mind, overcoming toxic people-pleasing, and healing grief.

I like books, music, museums, movies, theater. Science fiction and science fact. Chocolate. Took a test online that says I'm a "Pure Nerd." I don't like piña coladas and getting caught in the rain, but I do love fragrant flowers, skywatching at any hour of the day or night, palm trees, and romantic walks on the Malibu beach at sunset—oh, wait, that's all for a different kind of list.

Back to what I write about. I love dogs. I'm a nut for dogs of all shapes and kinds and sizes. For me, heaven is going to Central Park every morning with my cream colored Golden retriever named Sugar Bear and playing with the dozens of dogs we meet there on a regular basis. It's like the world's most fantastic dog show. You could sit on a bench and see an amazing parade of everything from teacup Chihuahuas to Great Danes the size of a horse, and all breeds and cross-breeds and Heinz 57 mutts in between. I am particularly drawn to furry dogs, the ones that shed all over you when you hug them, but they feel like big plush toys.

Over the years, I've had dogs as small as fifteen pounds (a Papillon named Irving) and as large as 115 (a Bernese Mountain Dog, Roxy).

Small, medium, large or giant, all dogs need to be cleaned up after.

The size of pooper scooper you need gets bigger and bigger the larger the breed.

For Trump's mess, we'll need an industrial size pooper scooper mounted on an 18-wheeler equipped with a back-up alarm.

Let's delve into the thinking process that Trump's voters were raised with, by looking at dog training and seeing what kind of insight comes to the surface.

We inadvertently create bullies and yappers and snappers out of our little dogs by picking them up when they misbehave, distracting them with treats, and petting them in an attempt to soothe their outrage at life.

Since childhood, I have had dogs in my life, and, seriously, no matter what size or breed or crossbreed the dog is, the issue of training is always up to the owner, not the dog.

Every dog owner/guardian should wear a sign "The buck stops here." There are no bad dogs, only dogs which have been overly pampered or seriously abused so that their innate nature of cooperating with man has been tampered with.

Years ago, when my daughter was a little girl, we had a Sheltie named Pippi Longstocking. She was a beautiful dog, just like a miniature Lassie. My late husband enrolled her in basic obedience classes, and then after she graduated that course, I took her to advanced training. Our daughter helped with the homework assignments as much as she could at that age. Pippi had been an 8-week-old surprise gift to our daughter that arrived just in time to enter in the Brownie Scout troop's pet show. Pippi won the blue ribbon for "Wiggliest Pet."

The advanced training class was held on Tuesday evenings one summer at Griffith Park in Hollywood. The area for the dog classes was immense, probably measurable in terms of acres. It took about ten minutes just to walk to the center of the field from the parking lot. When we got to the "off leash" exercise which was meant to demonstrate how well our dogs would sit in one place as we walked away from them, and then come when called, I bravely unclipped my dog's leash and told her to "Stay."

Pippi simply took off.

She sped across the vast park as if responding to the call of the wild and the scent of sheep and heather on the air.

Even though she'd never been outside of Los Angeles, somewhere in Pippi's DNA were her ancestors from the rugged Shetland Islands, part of Scotland in the northernmost part of the British Isles, where Shelties

(Shetland Sheepdogs) were traditionally working dogs rather than lap dogs.

I eventually caught up with her and returned to the class, shame-faced, knowing my lack of practice at home was the true reason for failing that lesson.

I doggedly taught Pippi hand signals and kept working with her on acceptable off-leash behavior, not as much as I could or should have, but eventually she did get better behaved over the years. Throughout her 16 years with us, she remained a yapper and an ankle nipper (typical of sheepdogs who have the genetic disposition to herd anything with legs).

Life with Pippi was fun and easy. She was affectionate, intelligent, sweet, and loved to fetch her tiny green football and bring it back for more.

But… as soon as I heard footsteps approaching the front door, and Pippi's ears perked up as she swiveled her head toward the entrance and prepared to leap, immediate panic overwhelmed me.

What would she do to show me up this time?

I dreaded social situations where I knew she was not going to be at her best. Embarrassed at the obvious implication that I hadn't trained her very well, I would pick her up and hold her when I answered the door, or when she lunged for guests' ankles.

Above all, I tried to distract her by petting and whispering soothing words, little knowing I was actually reinforcing her bad behavior and encouraging it to continue.

Her thinking must have been: *Hey! Let's bark at the doorbell every time, because that means treats and petting and being held! Woof woof woof! Yea, here come the treats!*

Years later when I was training our new Golden retriever puppy named Molly, I began to see the light about what I had done wrong with Pippi, who at that time was snapping at Molly's legs to the extent we had to keep the two dogs separated for many months until they settled into a state of amicable sibling-hood.

At first, I was able to scoop up Molly and, well, mollify her if she was misbehaving. But the tactics that worked with a little dog soon became impossible. Within a few weeks, I was unable to control her by picking her up—big dogs do get hefty fast, and Molly was at 40 pounds shortly after she was a dainty little pup I could cuddle in my arms. She eventually tipped the scales at 105 and that is not the size of dog you can simply drag along behind you.

Sometimes I envy those owners who have little dogs in their adorable matching harness-vests and leashes. My current Golden, Sugar Bear, and I see the little ones in Central Park and on Fifth Avenue every day. If the little dogs lunge at Sugar, they get picked up. If not, they get dragged along like a dust mop.

So now that you know a little of my lifetime history with dogs, let's look at dog training from the perspective of political parties and how people get there.

How do so many millions of Republicans get to the point where someone like Trump barks out: HATE who I tell you to hate, NOD when I tell you to nod, CLAP when I tell you to clap, VOTE for me when I tell you to vote... and they do it.

How did this happen? Is it a case of mass hypnosis?

The R-type of dog makes messes wherever it feels like, even in the House, and expects others to clean up after it when the stench becomes overwhelming. The R-type feels entitled to take what it wants. It loves to chase its own tail and pretend it is getting something accomplished.

We saw this coming. Republican anger has been stewing for a long time. Obamacare? No sense trying to explain to the Republicans what the Democrats have pointed out from the beginning – that it is the very same system as Republican Mitt Romney instituted when he was governor of Massachusetts.

Republicans see "Democrat" near any topic, and they instantly hate and deride it.

There is no logic to the labels Republicans apply to the issues.

But there is logic to how they turned out the way they have.

First, a quick look at history, because when schoolchildren learn that Abraham Lincoln was in the "Republican Party" I don't want them to have the misconception that means he would have voted for Donald Trump.

Mr. Trump is the opposite of all that President Lincoln stood for.

The Republicans have come very far indeed from the original tenets of their party platform. An historical document titled

"Republican Party Platform of 1860" contains 17 clauses, including one about admitting Kansas as a state. The document begins thus:

Resolved, That we, the delegated representatives of the Republican electors of the United States in Convention assembled, in discharge of the duty we owe to our constituents and our country, unite in the following declarations:

[I won't reproduce the entire document here, but these two clauses are of particular interest. The bold emphasis added is mine.]

2. That the maintenance of the principles promulgated in the Declaration of Independence and embodied in the Federal Constitution, **"That all men are created equal***; that they are endowed by their Creator with certain inalienable rights; that among these are life, liberty and the pursuit of happiness; that to secure these rights, governments are instituted among men, deriving their just powers from the consent of the governed," is essential to the preservation of our Republican institutions; and that the Federal Constitution, the Rights of the States, and the Union of the States must and shall be preserved…..*

14. That the **Republican party is opposed to any change in our naturalization laws or any state legislation by which the rights of citizens hitherto accorded to immigrants from foreign lands shall be abridged or impaired***; and in favor of giving a full and efficient protection to the rights of all classes of citizens, whether native or naturalized, both at home and abroad.*

****

Are you old enough or interested enough in American History to remember that the South was traditionally Democratic? Many "Red States" used to be "Blue States."

The change came in the 1960s with Civil Rights. Southern states did not want desegregation promulgated by the Democrats, and *en masse* they changed parties and voted Republican.

Revealing, isn't it? The party of Abraham Lincoln and The Emancipation Proclamation now harbored white elitists.

Where originally Republicans said no states should be allowed to do what they want (which apparently was what Democrats wanted back then), now the New Republicans demanded hands-off from the Federal government and wanted to be able to continue segregation on a state-by-state basis.

That takes us right back to the Civil War when the Union was divided because the Confederate States wanted slavery to be allowed on a state-by-state basis. Now that lessening of rights according to the color of your skin has been reinstituted by the Republican Party.

Basically the two parties switched places (not on all issues, however) and today's Democrats became the successors of Republican abolitionists and the new champions of Civil Rights.

Apparently, Republicans as a whole have the mindset of "my needs come first"—and anything that does not compute with that mindset is rejected out of hand before it even comes near the level of conscious awareness where one could examine an idea and decide whether to accept or reject it.

So let's see what kind of "humor" we can find for this section. I didn't promise this entire book would be a laugh-out-loud experience, but comedy does help us gain insight into the behavior of our fellow man and of our own behavior, so we can see where we have been and where we are headed more clearly than when we run into our dog crates and hide.

Picture this dog training class outside at a city park with tall leafy shade trees and a wide expanse of close-cropped grass or native plants.

There are two classes in session, one for large breeds, and the other for the miniatures, who would otherwise get trampled in the melee.

In the small dog class, the dogs leap and bark excitedly, the din is overwhelming. The owners feed them treats constantly in an effort to get them to listen to instructions.

When the dogs snap at each other and at the people and the instructor, the owners scoop up their little dogs, feed them more treats, give them lots of hugging and smooching to "settle down."

When it is time for the dog to learn to walk at heel, the owner yanks the dog along while the dog learns nothing, then gives it another treat, and again intervenes with hugs and pats if the dog yaps and snarls at the very notion of "obedience training."

What is that little dog learning?

Is it learning accountability for its own actions? Is it learning to behave nicely in society and with other dogs? Is it learning anything other than "It's not my fault!"... "I didn't do anything!" ... "The devil made me do it!"?

Is it learning that if you snap and snarl, others praise and reward you? If you demand more treats, you get them. If you don't like someone it's okay to hurl yourself at their legs and bite. If you defend your narrow life as being the only way to live, the only thing that happens is you get scooped up and given hugs and treats, and you get to continue thinking no one else counts.

If a big dog approaches, you are yanked away from it, snarling and growling, instead of being allowed to interact normally and actually find out you don't need to hate the big dogs because, actually, they have a lot to share with you and can be loads of fun, too.

Then, on the other side of the park, in the big dog class, the dogs are taught to sit when they are told to sit, to stay when they are asked to stay, to wait before jumping in or out of a car, to get "off" if they try to jump up on people, to lie down when they are told to lie down, to be quiet when they are barking too much, and to come when they are called.

They are taught to walk off-leash so they can enjoy the freedom of being a dog while not interfering with the freedoms of other dogs and their owners.

They learn that their rights end where another dog's rights begin.

They are taught "leave it!" if they try to take toys and treats and beds that do not belong to them.

They are happy to play with any dog, no matter its size, color or breed. Life is good!

What do you think these dogs are like to live with? They are the companions of life, the ones who make us smile and help us feel that life is about joy and helping one another and being kind to each other, about unconditional love and about sharing all the goodies of this planet with others instead of hogging them to ourselves.

The big dogs go on to further training to be seeing eye dogs for the blind, emotional support dogs for the traumatized, hospice and hospital dogs for the shut-ins, airport dogs for the stressed-out traveler, military and police dogs to assist their handlers in protecting citizens and in sniffing out drugs and dangerous substances (dogs are even trained to detect cancer by its smell, long before any scans will show its presence). They are our search and rescue dogs, and hearing ear dogs for the deaf and hearing impaired.

I met a Sheltie on the subway in NYC who had been trained to be a hearing ear dog—the perfect job for a bright animal with excellent hearing and affection for humans.

Of course, outside of this parable of the dog classes, little dogs and medium dogs and giant dogs all have the hearts of big dogs, and that is why you'll sometimes hear animal lovers say, "Dog Is My CoPilot."

Chapter 5

What Would Scooby Do?

In tough situations, people sometimes say, as a guideline for their own behavior: *What would God do? ... What would Jesus do? ... What would Love do?*

I asked: <u>What would Scooby do?</u>

For my international readers who may not be familiar with him, Scooby Doo is a cartoon Great Dane who is always getting into trouble in his adventures with his human friends, and growls "Ruh-Roh!" to mean "Uh-Oh!"

Our companion dogs across the land have been affected by the election results, and they sense the discord in Democratic families where relatives, or even spouses, actually voted for Trump. How does a family survive such a complete divide in philosophy?

There must be millions of mini-civil-wars going on all around us, and our pets are the hapless bystanders and absorbers of all that stress.

I decided it would be a good idea to find out more about this issue from the perspective of the dogs themselves. I hoped they would offer advice and feedback on how they still manage to cheerfully get up each day and lead a normal life despite all that is going on in the news.

If you've ever been around dogs, or observed their relationship to their family, you know how readily they pick up on the prevailing mood in the home. When voices are raised in anger, they find a way to slip off to safety. If tension is high, they whine and nudge you to be sure you are okay. When you are feeling low, they lay a head in your lap or place a paw on your knee and invite the patting which actually soothes and helps heal your mood.

I got the idea for this chapter's interview when I met a Golden retriever named Brinkley at Central Park and the very next day found out the name of a neighbor's Golden is Scooby. I was working on this book at the time, and so the meetings surely were serendipitous gifts from my Invisible Comedy Writing Team.

Who could resist setting up a recorded session with these two dogs and my own dear Golden?

When I decided to pose the question, "What would Scooby do?" I invited both Brinkley and Scooby to have a private conference with Sugar Bear.

Meet the panel:

Brinkley: A dark blonde Golden retriever male, age 2, fond of walks in the park; his favorite film is *You've Got Mail.*

Scooby: A russet-gold Golden retriever male, age 1, whose passion is meeting and greeting every tree within a three-block radius of home. He's still perfecting his "Ruh-Roh!" in honor of his namesake, Scooby Doo.

Sugar Bear: a cream-colored Golden retriever female, age 6, who has never met a person she didn't like. [She's never met Donald Trump or Steve Bannon and their tribe, and if it's up to me, she never will.]

I provided snacks, bowls of water, chew toys, and then let them get started.

I invited Brinkley to create his own interview questions, and then I simply sat nearby in the role of observer, and recorded the session.

Brinkley: Garr, ruff, wrr...?

Scooby: Rarah, ouch, oy vey!

Sugar Bear: Wara-wara, woo!

They immediately got up and helped themselves to the refreshments.

Startled by the brevity of the session, which was clearly over, I listened to the recording, trying to find a clue to what they had said.

When the dogs finished their snacks and settled on the floor for a nap, I realized my experiment had fallen flat. I listened to the recording once more, hoping to find a clue to crack the code.

And then I got an idea.

I prepared doggy bags of treats and tennis balls for Brinkley and Scooby, and then Sugar Bear and I escorted them to their separate homes. I've had two Goldens at the same time: the infamous Molly (whose name came about from our family comment, as we watched her wolf down her dinner and also Pippi's bowl of food, bowl and all, "Good golly, Miss Molly, don't eat it all!") and later on, after Pippi the Sheltie died, Peaches (a pale blonde Golden retriever) joined the household. I knew I'd be getting looks on Madison Avenue while walking three gorgeous, well-behaved Golden retrievers. We were stopped several times so the dogs could do their typical meet-and-greet with strangers.

While waiting for a light to change, I bent and asked the dogs if they wouldn't please share with me what they had said earlier.

They looked at me as if they didn't understand the question.

When Sugar Bear and I got home, I explained to her what I am about to tell you. She listened politely then curled up in her bed and resumed the nap I had interrupted a half hour earlier in order to take Scooby and Brinkley home.

While she was sleeping, I Skyped a ciphers expert and shared the recording with him. He asked to remain anonymous, apparently fearing his reputation might be affected if anyone found out what I had asked him to do.

He listened to the dogs' session several times, while making notes on a legal pad, but he finally shook his head. "It's not a cipher, not a code I can figure out."

"Then what is it?"

"I think... well, I think it's another language."

I sighed. "I like to believe I understand my dogs, but, to be honest, I don't really speak Dog. Do you, by any chance?"

He replied that he had five cats, so we ended the call.

I tried to accept that the experiment had been a waste of time, other than, of course, being loads of fun to hang out with two more Goldens.

However, later that evening, while watching *Star Trek* reruns on Netflix, I remembered meeting someone who might be able to help me.

Years ago, when I lived in Hollywood in the Sunset Hills above the Chateau Marmont, I was driving home from work at Max Factor, where I was in the marketing department at the company's world headquarters, heading west on Hollywood Boulevard, driving in the left-hand lane, approaching the signal at Laurel Canyon Boulevard.

I saw a convertible coming up on my right and realized the driver was Captain Kirk – William Shatner. When you live in Los Angeles, you become at least somewhat accustomed to spotting famous actors and directors around town.

To act like a cool local, you never ever wave and grin and call out their name like some rube. You do your best to act blasé while secretly goggling at them like any star struck tourist would. This was long before cell phones and camera apps, so I didn't get a photo of him. I figure it would've been all wobbly and blurry anyway, taken from a moving vehicle and trying to focus on another moving vehicle.

I was a big Star Trek fan, and still am, so you can imagine my dilemma. Here was a golden opportunity – Kirk just a few feet away! -- and if I let my innate sense of shyness and propriety keep me quiet, I'd blow it. I didn't want this to be one of those regrets that we all end up with when we don't do something and later wish we had.

So I mustered up my gumption, smiled and waved. "Hi," I called out eloquently, glad that the windows were down in my car and the top down in his.

Without missing a beat, he waved an arm in the air and yelled out to me, "Hi, Elaine!"

And then we were both turning right onto Laurel Canyon but he waved a cheery goodbye, and then sped off toward the Valley. I did a U-turn where you are able to head the other way and then continue up into the hills on Hollywood

Boulevard where it is all residential.

Wow. Captain Kirk knew my name. Sort of. It wasn't the first time I'd been called Elaine, and probably won't be the last. Even a neighbor who had known me for several years introduced me as "Elaine" to all the other guests at his dinner party. He was so firmly insistent about it that I stopped correcting him after the first twenty minutes and even began introducing myself as Elaine, just to keep the peace.

Was this my parents' fault? Did they put the wrong name on my birth certificate when they wrote "Evelyn"? Am I actually an "Elaine" going through life under an alias? Perhaps I'll never know the answer.

Another thing about Los Angeles is that networking contacts never die. You hold onto them forever no matter how tenuous the connection is. If you see someone crossing the street, later on you can tell them, "Hey, good to see you again! Remember that time we met near the corner of Sunset Boulevard and Crescent Heights?"

So now I decided to trade on my connection with William Shatner.

Moments later I was on a Skype call with him. Oddly enough he recognized me immediately. You see? Blondes really do have more fun.

Bill: "Hey, Elaine, good to see you!"

Me: "Um, it's 'Evelyn' but that's okay. Good to see you, too."

Bill: "Seems like it's been a while. When—"

I didn't want to tell him that when we "met" he was working on *Star Trek: The Motion Picture* and was probably on his way home from Paramount Studios when I saw him.

Me: "Time is relative, isn't it?"

Bill: "You still living in Hollywood?"

Me: "I'll be back someday, but for now I'm in Manhattan. Listen, I don't want to keep you, but I have a little favor to ask."

Bill: "Anything for you."

I really do wish I knew who he thought I was. I mean, is there an "Elaine" out there who is still waiting for him to call, but he's been thinking of me all this time?

I told him what I wanted, and we ended the Skype call with mutual promises to stay in touch.

10 seconds later, there was a shimmer of light on the table next to my computer, and a Universal Translator device materialized at the precise coordinates I had given him.

Normally, the Universal Translator is used for real-time communication, and processes language by a brainwave scan.

Since I had already taken Brinkley and Scooby home, I hoped the recording would suffice. Kirk, I mean Bill Shatner, had assured me it would.

I immediately got to work translating the dog conference.

Here is the result:

Brinkley: Garr, ruff, wrr...? [*How's it hangin', Scoob?*]

Scooby: Rarah, ouch, oy vey! [*Don't mention that! Stitches come out Monday.*]

Sugar Bear: Wara-wara, woo! [*La-la-la! I can't hear you!*]

I guess even with dogs, life goes on, and the everyday ups and downs, and trips to the vet for getting neutered take over their conversations with friends when they're just hanging out at home.

While using the translator, I got another idea. That's one of the things I do best. When I took the *Strengths Finder 2.0* questionnaire a few years ago, they ranked my top five natural talents and mental strengths. Number one was "Ideation." Basically, I'm an idea person. Ideas love me and I love them.

So when I contacted Bill Shatner a few minutes later – to give him the new coordinates for the Universal Translator so he could zap it back to wherever it is normally stored, having promised I would not take the translator device outside or use it for any other purpose – I broached my latest idea.

He began nodding.

Bill: "You had me at 'You're the only one who can do this.' Such a cajoler!"

Me: "I really think this would work. Insurance companies call it a 'mysterious disappearance' when an item of jewelry goes missing, so probably nobody would ever think of coming after you. Just—"

He tried to interrupt, but I was too nervous he'd say "No" to my plan, so I hurtled ahead.

Me: "—keep a lock on certain life forms and when they're all together in the Oval Office at the same time, just beam them out to another galaxy where they can't do any more harm and—"

Bill: "Don't say another word. Please."

My shoulders slumped. He wasn't interested after all, wouldn't even let me finish. I knew it was a great idea, one that would help so many millions of people. And yet I'd been unsuccessful in my bid to convince the one person in the universe who could save the Federation, er, the United States.

But then he gave me a wink and lowered his voice to a whisper.

Bill: "It's already in the works. See ya soon, Elaine. Kirk out."

Chapter 6

Trump vs Trump (a skit à la SNL)

TRUMP VS TRUMP

"The Looking Glass"

A television skit

written by

Evelyn Roberts Brooks

THE WRITER'S DREAM CAST

DONALD .... ALEC BALDWIN
MIRROR TRUMP .... MERYL STREEP

RUSSIAN MAID .... DAN AYKROYD

GUEST CAST
VIA VIDEO MONTAGE

PROTESTORS...........MILLIONS OF REAL PEOPLE
FADE IN:

<u>INT. DONALD'S DRESSING ROOM - NIGHT (A
SATURDAY)</u>

DONALD IS GETTING DRESSED TO GO OUT,
TRYING ON SEVERAL SLIGHTLY DIFFERENT RED
TIES IN FRONT OF A LOOKING GLASS.

                    DONALD
          (AFTER A MOMENT) Red, red, red.
          Yep, red is my excellent choice.

FROM INSIDE THE LOOKING GLASS, MIRROR
TRUMP SCOWLS.

                  MIRROR TRUMP
             If you've finished primping,
           could we get back to our speech?

DONALD CHANGES HIS TIE AGAIN, DURING:

62

                    DONALD
             Blah, blah, blah, blah.

MIRROR TRUMP IS NOT AMUSED.

                  MIRROR TRUMP
             Then we'll start at the top.

DONALD'S RUSSIAN MAID ENTERS WITH A BOWL
OF BORSCHT ON A SILVER TRAY.

                  RUSSIAN MAID
             Drink your borscht! Da!

                    DONALD
                 Borscht? Nyet!

DONALD TOSSES THE SOUP INTO A POTTED
PALM, TURNS BACK TO THE MIRROR.

                DONALD (CONT'D)
         Another speech? Can't I use cue cards?

BEHIND DONALD, THE PALM TREE SHUDDERS.
THE MAID SWILLS FROM A VODKA BOTTLE.

                  MIRROR TRUMP
         You're supposed to know our position on
                all the issues by rote.
               (OFF HIS CONFUSION)
             That means memorize it.

DONALD
Okay, shoot... Oops.
(NERVOUS LAUGH)
Guess I shouldn't invite that.
Bad karma or something.

THE MAID BUSTLES ABOUT, PICKING UP SHIRTS
AND TIES, GUZZLING VODKA, DUSTING THE
DOG AND THE GOLDFISH.

SHE TURNS, REVEALING THE BACK OF HER
SHIRT: "I [HEART] PUTIN."

MIRROR TRUMP
(RELENTLESS, TO DONALD)
Start. At. The. Top.

DONALD SMOOTHS HIS COMBOVER WITH A
QUESTIONING LOOK.

MIRROR TRUMP (CONT'D)
The top. Of our speech.
That means the beginning.

DONALD
You keep staring. What?
(PEERS CLOSER, EXAMINES HIS TEETH,
SUCKING AND GRIMACING)

Do I still have spinach in my teeth from lunch?

MIRROR TRUMP RECOILS, FANS AWAY A BAD ODOR.

MIRROR TRUMP
No more garlic for you...
Your lines? What we rehearsed
this afternoon before your three-hour nap?

DONALD
Uh...

MIRROR TRUMP
Once more, from the t—
(CATCHING ITSELF)
from the start.
What's our position on Climate Change?

DONALD BRIGHTENS. HE KNOWS THIS ONE.

DONALD
The Mexicans invented Climate Change
so they can raise the price on avocados.

SEEING MIRROR TRUMP'S PURSED LIPS, DONALD POINTS TO A WISP OF HAIR STICKING UP, QUESTIONING.

MIRROR TRUMP SHAKES ITS HEAD, LONG-

SUFFERING.

DONALD REACHES FOR AN INDUSTRIAL-SIZE POWER SPRAYER MARKED "EXTRA-HOLD." SPRAYS HIS COMBOVER DURING:

MIRROR TRUMP
The Chinese invented Climate Change.
So they can steal more jobs from
America's blue collar workers.
You are going to bring back those
jobs from China. Remember?
You're not, of course, but it sounds good.

DONALD
(DUTIFULLY) I am going to…
Wait. If the Chinese are the ones
growing the avocados now, won't
they get bruised in those
big shipping containers?
I hate when guacamole turns
brown! I don't want my—

MIRROR TRUMP
(TRIES TO STOP THE RANT) Let's focus—

DONALD
--guacamole turning brown from being
smashed by the stupid Chinese!

MIRROR TRUMP
Stop fussing with our combover.

Any more hair spray and your head
will ignite if someone thinks the word "fire."

DONALD POUTS, GIVES A FINAL BLAST TO HIS
HAIR, TURNS OFF THE SPRAYER.

BEHIND DONALD, THE CURTAINS, THE DOG, THE
GOLDFISH AND THE RUSSIAN MAID ARE FROZEN
STIFF FROM THE OVERSPRAY.

> MIRROR TRUMP (CONT'D)
> Back to the agenda.
> What is our position on Civil Rights?

> DONALD
> (SMIRKS, CONFIDENT)
> We already have all the rights
> we need in the Bill of Rights.

> MIRROR TRUMP
> (PROMPTING) Which is...?

> DONALD
> In the Declaration of In—

> MIRROR TRUMP
> [SOTTO] The first ten amendments
> to the United States Constitution.

DONALD

Yeah, that's what I said. And it's ah,
well, the Bill of Rights is like a, you know,
a kind of bill, like from the dry
cleaners, saying what you can and
can't do, like, uh, not being
responsible for buttons that fall off
or sequins and feathers.

MIRROR TRUMP

Don't mention sequins again.
Okay, Donald? That's the
third time today.

DONALD

(GRUMBLING) I like sequins.
They're all sparkly and shiny.
I'm gonna have the White House
covered in sequins and...
(GETTING MORE AND MORE
EXCITED) and gold foil trim
around the windows! And my sign
on top of the whole building,
the one that's gonna say
"Trump Lives Here"--that's
gonna be in DIAMONDS!

MIRROR TRUMP TAPS THE GLASS TO GET HIS
ATTENTION.

MIRROR TRUMP
(HARSH) Dakota Pipeline?

DONALD BARKS OUT THE ANSWERS:

DONALD
Drill 'em!

MIRROR TRUMP
Walls against immigrants?

DONALD
Build 'em!

MIRROR TRUMP
Affordable education?

DONALD
Home school 'em!

MIRROR TRUMP
Health care?

DONALD
Ignore 'em!

MIRROR TRUMP
Social Security and Medicare?

DONALD
Euthanize 'em!

MIRROR TRUMP
Scientists?

DONALD
Fire 'em!

MIRROR TRUMP
Women?

DONALD
Fuck 'em!

MIRROR TRUMP SMOOTHS A HAND OVER ITS
COMBOVER. NODS, COLDLY SATISFIED: AS GOOD
AS IT GETS.

DONALD (CONT'D)
(WORRIED) But what about
my guacamole? Will I still be able
to get avocados?

MIRROR TRUMP
Of course, Donald. You'll fly them
in on Air Force One -- right over
the Mexican Wall.

FADE TO BLACK.

FADE UP ON:

A VIDEO MONTAGE:

EXT. CITIES AND TOWNS AROUND THE WORLD - DAY
PAN THE GLOBE.

STARTING WITH WASHINGTON, D.C., ZOOM IN ON MILLIONS OF TRUMP PROTESTERS AND MARCHERS IN BIG CITIES AND SMALL.

THE PROTESTORS CARRY SIGNS SUCH AS:
LOVE TRUMPS HATE;
WOMEN'S RIGHTS ARE HUMAN RIGHTS;
NO BAN NO WALL NO RAIDS;
KEEP YOUR HANDS OFF MY MAMMOGRAMS;
STAND INDIVISIBLE;
DEMOCRACY LIVES;
JOIN THE RESISTANCE;
BE A FREEDOM FIGHTER.
FADE OUT.

Chapter 7

No One Forced Republicans to Vote for Trump

If you've never lived in or visited New York City, you may not know this factoid about it: there are spitters here. Lots of them. Upon moving here, I didn't understand at first why there were so many signs warning people not to spit. But then, immediately, I started seeing spitters in action. Never, ever, walk barefooted in the city. Seriously, the sidewalk is covered with blobs of phlegm. People don't spit in the trash cans or in the street. They spit on the sidewalk, whether you are in their way or not.

One day, I actually witnessed a father instructing his son on the proper way to spit.

I had just crossed a major street, coming from the library, and saw a boy about thirteen starting to spit into his hand. The father pushed the boy's hand away and pointed to the sidewalk. "SPIT! Never spit into your own hand! Spit on the sidewalk!" The curb was about two steps away from them, but no, even the street was apparently not the correct place to spit according to that father. I suddenly pictured generation after generation in that family, all the dads teaching the sons how to spit on the sidewalks of New York.

And while we're on the topic of Monkey See, Monkey Do – please don't let your kids (or yourself) inadvertently imitate the Trump Scowl. While writing this chapter, taking a break to walk Sugar Bear, a couple loped towards us, their heads lowered, talking. They were both scowling so hard they had uni-brows because of the anger lines squishing their eyes together. Not an attractive look for anyone.

I'm not sure if I can do a good job making the rest of this chapter even remotely funny, so I won't try. The 2016 election outcome means too much to me to be flippant about, but I didn't want to lead off with a discussion of "why" Republicans did what they did, so that's why I told you about the whole spitting-in-the-city behavior. The spitting is disgusting to me; seriously, you frequently have to jump out of the way or sidestep this spitting segment of the population, and so is the result of the 2016 presidential election. That's the tie-in.

I keep reminding myself that when a situation is really bad, that means there is an opposite waiting for us, that is really wonderful—our job is to call it to us like we've attached a tractor beam and are reeling it in with the law of attraction in action.

Our hard-won and much-envied secret ballot system in the

USA allows a person to change their mind even at the last moment, and never have to tell another soul that they voted for someone else instead.

This is not a Third World country where you vote at risk of your life. Where you must stand in line for days (well, okay, yeah, due to Republican shenanigans in more than one election, Democratic voters were forced to stand in very long lines, but even the Republicans in Florida and elsewhere stopped shy of having soldiers with machine guns trained on voters to intimidate them.)

We always have a choice.

Even if someone holds a gun to your head and orders you to do something abhorrent, you still have a choice.

From the outside, it appears as if Trump's supporters were brainwashed.

There were 60-odd million Trump voters.

Here are the options I see, on a brief analysis of the "average" Trump voter (meaning we exclude Trump's handlers and advisors and foreign puppeteers and Wall Street cronies):

A. This type of voter didn't bother to look past the end of his/her nose to find out more about his/her Party Candidate.

B. This type of voter heard or saw or read some unpleasant things about Trump but ignored those things. After all,

Trump was the Republican Party Candidate so he must be the correct choice.

C. This type of voter knew exactly who Trump was and what he represented, and approved. Fanatically.

D. This type of voter decided Trump's "faults" could be overlooked because there was something he wanted above all: A republican in the White House – correction: A white male Republican in the White House.

E. This type of voter was so angry about his own life that he resonated with Trump's platform of anger and retaliation, and didn't look any further to see what would really happen with a corrupt man like Trump in the White House.

I believe most Republicans were operating out of an old paradigm when they voted for Donald Trump, a mindset of anger that has gotten stronger and more entrenched generation after generation.

There even seems to be an attitude post-election where those voters who recognize belatedly what a disastrous choice Trump was still stand by him because he's the Republican in office now. They are so restricted in their thinking that they can't break away from a feudal system of fealty to the party leaders.

How many millions of Trump's voters really agree That Man was the best choice for President of a country they claim to love, that they pledge allegiance to?

A Man who doesn't hide his contempt for women, for the disabled, for people whose skin is not what is called "white."

A Man who further demonstrates his ignorance and inexperience regarding diplomacy and foreign policy by ranting, "I've been places!"

A Man who stirs up the hatred of people who claim to be followers of the metaphysical teacher Jesus Christ.

Let me digress for a moment about extreme "Evangelical Christians" in America today. I don't get it. I was raised Catholic, and we were taught about charitable acts and the brotherhood of man and Civil Rights.

Who are these Evangelical extremists? I don't think "all" Christians in America approve of Donald Trump, but he certainly has appeal for the extremists who are full of righteousness that they are the only ones worth considering when laws are being written and passed.

Over two thousand years ago, the teacher called Jesus Christ brought earthshaking advice to humanity: LOVE THY BROTHER. That revolutionary message was intended to replace the Old Testament creed of revenge, "an eye for an eye, a tooth for a tooth," and was so radical the political leaders had to kill Jesus to try to shut him up. But about fifty years later, people began writing about Jesus and sharing the messages that had been handed down, until they had a book called the New Testament.

Testament: evidence, witness.

Back to Donald Trump, because I'm not finished with my summary of him (I could go on for pages, but I only want to put a few facts out in front of you while we look at what's going on.)

A typical comment of narcissists and egomaniacs is "The masses are asses," and Donald Trump demonstrates that outlook on a daily basis.

Did Trump's voters really look at his overwhelming lack of qualifications and say, "No big deal. It's okay"?

I am aware of reports that some Republicans, particularly Republican women, refused to vote for Donald Trump. They were brave. They were not willing to compromise their core values and deliberately choose a misogynist and racist to be leader of the free world. That is why, throughout this book I often use the term "Trump voters" instead of "Republicans." But seriously, if you didn't agree with your party's selection of Trump as your candidate, why did you stay in the party?

Guess what else Mr. Trump has done for America? From the viewpoint of the rest of the world, The United States is no longer leader of the free world. Our nation is a sick joke, because of Trump.

The selection of Donald Trump during the Republican Convention shocked many Republicans, and of course was mindboggling to Democrats. A man who has never held even a minor political position such as a township council member? A man whose foreign experience is investing, pillaging for profits, and then hiding behind his lawyers?

Bottom Line: REPUBLICANS DIDN'T HAVE TO VOTE FOR DONALD TRUMP.

But they did, in large enough numbers to amass enough Electoral Votes to steal the win from the People's Choice, Hillary Clinton.

In my opinion, the stakes were the highest they've been in a long time, and yet the voter turnout was the lowest in 20 years.

I think a big part of it is the Electoral College system. Common reactions might be:

--Why should I bother to vote? I live in a Red State and I'm a Democrat and I know the Republicans will get my state's allotted electoral votes.

--Why should I bother? I live in a Blue State and I'm a Democrat so I don't need to show up. There are plenty of people without me and the Democrats will get the electoral votes.

Millions of people in America believed, rightly so, that their single vote might not make any difference at all.

The Electoral College system must be abandoned. Considering that Trump is already working on his re-election campaign and his first month in office is barely over at this writing, we can bet he won't volunteer to dismantle the Electoral College that allowed him to be elected in the first place, despite not having the most votes.

How did Trump get elected? Because he manipulated hate and anger and fear, and not enough people knew how to combat the assault of that kind of mental energy or force field.

In the musical *South Pacific*, we are reminded that racism of all varieties is taught to children. The children don't come up with these ideas on their own, they learn them at home and at school and from their community.

"You've got to be carefully taught" is a line from one of the songs. And I think of it when I eavesdrop on conversations where people are complaining about everything in their life no matter how trivial. They were taught that complaining habit, and they continued practicing it until it is so entrenched in their outlook that they have a very difficult time accepting new ideas such as positive affirmations, and voting to help others even if you won't get anything out of the new regulation yourself.

Chapter 8

Broken American Flag

Whenever I am deep into writing a new book or screenplay, the project consumes my thoughts, and I often wake in the night to grab a pad of paper and frantically scribble ideas and dialogue that flow so effortlessly and creatively as soon as I am away from my computer or have nothing to write with.

Having read at some point that turning on a light actually triggers waking up, I carefully avoid doing so, hoping I'll be able to go back to sleep after honoring my muses by capturing the wonderful ideas they send me.

Unfortunately, the logic of this always fails:

1. Even though I'm only half sitting up, and still under the covers, I'm already awake while I'm writing in the dark. At this point, there's little chance that even a spotlight shined in my eyes for the Third Degree treatment in a *film noir* would make me more awake than turning on a tiny night light so I actually could see what I was writing.

2. In my haste to get down the ideas that are coming in faster than a speeding bullet, my handwriting becomes practically illegible. Worse than a doctor's. Making matters worse, when

I flip to a blank sheet before the ideas escape into the ether, I lose track whether or not I already wrote on the back of that page—so I frequently end up being confronted in the morning with pages of undecipherable writing and sheets that have been written on top to bottom, twice.

It's like trying to separate out the images of a double-exposure from the old style cameras where the roll of film didn't get replaced with a fresh one but inadvertently got wound again inside the camera, and reused. You send the film out to be developed and then pick up a packet of prints that have double images. Thus you have pictures of a community picnic with people you barely even know superimposed on priceless shots of your once-in-a-lifetime vacation cruise.

Before I tell you about my flag dream, I should admit that even though I may end up awake for a few hours in the middle of the night, I invariably fall asleep again, and that is when I usually have a really vivid, colorful dream that is worthy of the big screen.

This chapter originally included a rather lengthy explanation of an insomniac cure that I came up with some months ago and have been longing to insert into one of my books, but it never seems to belong. And, to be honest, it didn't belong here either. It made the chapter too long.

In addition, each time I lovingly polished the insomnia section, I kept getting this image of Albert Einstein sticking his tongue out at me and shaking his head "No." That was a pretty clear indication that I should edit it out. As an alternative, I decided to post the "Prime Numbers Insomnia Cure" article at my website. You can find it here.

One of the big challenges my sleeptime and I face on a regular basis, as if insomnia and I are on this road of life joined at the hip, is if when one of my dogs needs to go out in the middle of the night, it's almost impossible for me to fall back asleep. I usually end up reading for a couple of hours and sometimes am lucky enough to fall back asleep just about the time I should be getting up.

On this particular night, Sugar Bear got me up at 4am. Apparently she'd heard another dog shout *Hello* from down the street and wanted to go outside to check things out.

For Christmas the prior year, I had made the mistake of giving her a DVD of "101 Dalmatians" which she watches all the time. Because of it, she's alert to the idea of sharing long-distance messages with other dogs such as: "101 puppies have been stolen! Watch out for a deranged, skinny woman with skunk hair!"

Apparently the message being barked across New York City– East Side, West Side, All Around the Town—was: "No Bans! No Walls! No Raids! Free Speech!"

When we got back inside that night, Sugar Bear happily curled up in her bed, clearly feeling she had done her duty as a protestor for one day at least, and was soon snoring softly, while I tried desperately to recapture a state of sleep.

I gave up at 5am, opened my iPad—with the brightness setting as low as possible, again, for that whole don't-trigger-the melatonin-wake-up thing —and finished reading a WW2 espionage mystery.

Yawn. Hoping the yawn meant sleep was nigh, I hastily closed my iPad, yanked on my eye mask and scrunched under the covers. By then it was after 6am. But I slept, and I dreamt. In color.

All too soon, about an hour later, Sugar Bear woke me with a silent but intense reminder that it was time to leave for our morning walk in Central Park, where the off-leash hours for dogs is 6am-9am and the rest of the time they must be leashed.

I don't know the off-leash hours for humans but the park is closed 1am-6am daily.

Sugar Bear's preferred method of waking me is to stand next to me and breathe quietly, with her mouth about 1 inch from my nose. That blast of warm air gets my attention, especially since her diet is primarily salmon.

Still, her fish breath is far better than the outgassing method that some big dogs seem to delight in expressing.

I told Sugar Bear about the dream I was having, hoping she would help me interpret it:

I was sitting at a workbench, with the normal clutter of tools, nails, screws, and half-finished projects. I was trying to mend a pair of broken kitchen scissors with glue. The scissors had somehow come apart into two halves, and pieces of the handles were missing. The design on the handles created the American flag, but only when the scissors were properly closed.

(Seriously, this was my dream while writing this book.)

I searched drawers for the missing bits and only found a few flakes of red, white and blue paint. I got the scissor halves fastened in the middle and tested: open, shut. Yes, they were working again although they weren't perfect. My late husband leaned over my shoulder and rummaged in a drawer for flag pieces, but no luck.

Sugar Bear, who knows how much I love America, told me the dream was about post-election 2017, where the two parts of red and blue cannot quite be mended to be whole, but we can keep searching for ways to make the scissors work anyway...and cut away the things that are harmful to our nation.

I don't know if I'll live to see a day when those halves of the American flag scissors are truly mended, but I do know this:

Every day, in every way possible, I'll do my best to be part of the solution—part of the glue, part of the healing, part of the progressive realization of this very worthy ideal known as the United States of America, land of the free and home of the brave.

"Success is the progressive realization
of a worthy ideal."

Earl Nightingale

Chapter 9

Rump Voters & Magical Thinking

Um, I meant to type "Trump" not "Rump," which, as we all know, is a mammal's ass. When you go to the meat counter to buy a roast from the hindquarters of the animal, they sell you a "rump roast" not a "trump roast."

(I actually did miss the "T" while typing the chapter title, and since I laughed when I noticed my typo I decided to keep it, in the hope you might get a delicious little chuckle, too.)

Magical thinking is when you look at what is happening and hear what someone is saying, but instead of THINKING and becoming aware of what it really means, you ignore the subtext and re-interpret the situation to fit what you want it to be.

Little kids do this all the time. They break a vase and say someone else did it, not because they are deliberately lying but because that is what they <u>wish</u> had happened. *Not me! I didn't do it! It was broken when I got here!*

Thus, we have people who should've known better than to

believe in a corrupt businessman who promised to bring overseas jobs back to American workers, who promised until his face was bright red that he would improve the economy. But they believed anyway, because they wished it was all true.

Here's some of the magical thinking indulged in by Rump Voters, as exemplified for us in several movies that ... well, take a look and decide for yourself whether my choices are apt or not:

HE'LL BRING BACK WHITE "CHRISTIAN" AMERICA

Hilly Holbrook (Bryce Dallas Howard): They carry different diseases than we do. That's why I've drafted the Home Health Sanitation Initiative.

Eugenia 'Skeeter' Phelan (Emma Stone): The what?

Hilly Holbrook: A disease-preventative bill that requires every white home to have a separate bathroom for the colored help. It's been endorsed by the White Citizen's Council.

Eugenia 'Skeeter' Phelan: Maybe we should just build <u>you</u> a bathroom outside, Hilly.

from *The Help* (2011) written by Tate Taylor based on the novel by Kathryn Stockett

HIS FAME WILL RUB OFF ON ME

Navin R. Johnson (Steve Martin): The new phone book's here! The new phone book's here!

Harry Hartounian (Jackie Mason): Boy, I wish I could get that excited about nothing.

Navin R. Johnson: Nothing? Are you kidding? Page 73 - Johnson, Navin R.! I'm somebody now! Millions of people look at this book every day! This is the kind of spontaneous publicity - your name in print - that makes people. I'm in print! Things are going to start happening to me now.

from *The Jerk* (1979) written by Steve Martin

TRUMP'S A TV STAR–HE KNOWS HOW TO GET $@!# DONE!

Howard Beale (Peter Finch): Right now, there is a whole, an entire generation that never knew anything that didn't come out of this tube. This tube is the gospel, the ultimate revelation; this tube can make or break presidents, popes, prime ministers; this tube is the most awesome goddamn propaganda force in the whole godless world, and woe is us if it ever falls into the hands of the wrong people, and that's why woe is us that Edward George Ruddy died. Because this company is now in the hands of CCA, the Communications Corporation of America; there's a new chairman of the board, a man called Frank Hackett, sitting in Mr. Ruddy's office on the twentieth floor. And when the 12th largest company in the world controls the most awesome goddamn propaganda force in the whole godless world, who knows what shit will be peddled for truth on this network?

from *Network* (1976) written by Paddy Chayefsky

THE MONEY WILL TRICKLE DOWN TO ME

Lawrence Garfield (Danny DeVito): I love money. I love money more than the things it can buy. There's only one thing I love more than money. You know what that is? OTHER PEOPLE'S MONEY.

from *Other People's Money* (1991) written by Alvin Sargent based on the play by Jerry Sterner

MY FACTORY JOB WILL COME BACK FROM CHINA

Tom Granick (William Hurt): Just remember that you're not just reading the news, you're narrating it. Everybody has to sell a little. You're selling them this idea of you, you know, you're sort of saying, trust me I'm, um, credible. So when you feel yourself just reading, stop! Start selling a little.

from *Broadcast News* (1987) written by James L. Brooks

HE'S MY PARTY'S CANDIDATE SO HE'S THE BEST CHOICE

Don Corleone (Marlon Brando): I have a sentimental weakness for my children and I spoil them, as you can see. They talk when they should listen. Anyway, Signor Sollozzo, my no to you is final. I want to congratulate you on your new business and I'm sure you'll do very well and good luck to you. Especially since your interests don't conflict with mine. Thank you.

from *The Godfather* (1972) written by Mario Puzo and Francis

Ford Coppola

IT DOESN'T MATTER IF HE'S QUALIFIED, HE'LL DO A GREAT JOB

The Colonel (Walter Brennan): I don't read no papers, and I don't listen to radios either. I know the world's been shaved by a drunken barber, and I don't have to read it.

from *Meet John Doe* (1940) written by Robert Riskin, based on a story by Richard Connell and Robert Presnell.

HYPNOTIZED BY TRUMP'S SOUNDBITES

Detective Krevoy (Richard Tyson): Well, uh, can you tell us his name?

Ted (Ben Stiller): Ah... no, I didn't catch it. Can we cut to the chase, I mean, am I like in a lot of trouble here?

Detective Stabler: [nods] First tell us why you did it.

Ted: Why I did it? Ah... I don't know. Boredom? The guy turned to be a blubber mouth who just would not shut up.

from *There's Something About Mary* (1998) written by Ed Decter & John J. Strauss and Peter Farrelly & Bobby Farrelly

Chapter 10

"But I Thought You Said"

Have you ever been chatting with a friend, each of you earnestly talking about something and yet there's a frustration filling the air as you grow more confused or even annoyed, only to discover, hopefully with laughter, that you were each talking about something totally different?

It happens all the time.

You think your friend said one thing, but she said something else—and you were thinking your own thoughts and only heard part of it, or assumed you were discussing the same aspect of a situation and responded to that.

I'm reminded of a book series that was a favorite of mine growing up and that I shared with my daughter, too. In this particular volume in the series, *Mrs. Piggle-Wiggle's Magic* by Betty MacDonald, the iconic Mrs. Piggle-Wiggle helps Mr. and Mrs. Burbank whose children have a bad case of "I-Thought-You-Said-itis."

In the "Thought-You-Saiders Cure" the children who bring

cinnamon rolls from the kitchen instead of the sugar bowl explain away their misbehavior by protesting, "But I thought you said…"

In the end, Mrs. Piggle-Wiggle gives the parents a magical powder to sprinkle in the children's ears while they are sleeping. It works perfectly! The next morning, communication and family harmony are restored.

We need a magical cure, too.

I know many of us are still hoping to wake up and find it was all a nightmare, and Trump isn't really the president.

So I began thinking…

What if a lot of the differences between Democrats and the average Republicans are a matter of needing a magic powder to cure faulty listening?

"But I thought you said –" are words that can lead to greater understanding, or to a wider gulf. It all depends on how both sides are willing to discuss things.

Will it be an open discussion?

Or will one of the parties say one thing in public and then in secret do the exact opposite? That's the case today with the Trump administration—the secret deals started during the campaign and escalated on Day One of his taking over the White House.

But when it comes to the health and wellbeing of an entire nation and by extension the rest of the world, it's not so funny.

What could some of those misunderstandings be, if only the world were as easily cured of its ills as in a Mrs. Piggle-Wiggle tale for children?

What if it's just a simple case of not hearing what the other person said?

~~~

Republican: "I thought you said we'll see an avalanche from his money wagon!"

Democrat: "No, I said we'll see an avalanche from his HONEY WAGON!"

[A "honey wagon" is a portable toilet.]

~~~

Republican: "I thought you said Trump was a grateful kinda guy."

Democrat: "No, I said he's a HATEFUL kind of guy!"

~~~

Republican: "I thought you said if he gets in, the jobs will flow."

Democrat: "No, I said IF HE GETS IN, MORE JOBS WILL GO!"

~~~

Republican: "I thought you said Trump could use a few hugs."

Democrat: "No, I said he acts like he uses DRUGS!"

~~~

Republican: "I thought you said you're looking forward to meeting him."

Democrat: "No, I said I'M LOOKING FORWARD TO DEFEATING HIM!"

~~~

Republican: "I thought you said he looks like a baseball hitter."

Democrat: "No, I said he's like a RACIST, TALL HITLER!"

~~~

Republican: "I thought you said he's a Muppet to gush on."

Democrat: "No, I said he's a PUPPET OF RUSSIA!"

~~~

Republican: "I thought you said Trump's the plain choice."

Democrat: "No, I said he's a COMPLAINER'S CHOICE!"

~~~

Republican: "I thought you said he comes in a car that's black and nifty."

Democrat: "No, I said WE'VE COME TOO FAR TO GO BACK TO THE FIFTIES!"

~~~

Republican: "I thought you said he's the high quality kind of man this country needs."

Democrat: "No, I said he's the LEAST QUALIFIED CANDIDATE, WITH A HISTORY OF GREED!"

~~~

Republican: "I thought you said he thinks he's a big Care Bear."

Democrat: "No, I said HE THINKS HE'S A BIG EMPEROR!"

~~~

Republican: "I thought you said he's afraid of whirled peas."

Democrat: "No, I said HE'S A THREAT TO WORLD

PEACE!"

~~~

Republican: "I thought you said the strategy was to vote for Trump."

Democrat: "No, I said it would be a <u>TRAGEDY</u> to vote for Trump."

~~~

Humor aside, if there was a way to turn the clock back until the calendar date was Election Day 2016, what, if anything, would you do differently?

Would you invite friends to join you at the polls—friends who had said they weren't going to bother to vote because it wouldn't really matter who won?

Mr. Trump is already planning his re-election.

Let's start thinking now about 2020, and envision what we want: a sensible Democrat in the White House.

We can't be "against" Donald Trump because that energizes his campaign.

What will we do differently? How can we invite more people into the sensible choice of the progressive Democratic platform that, flaws and all, means moving forward with liberty and justice for all, not just a few? Let's find the ways.

Chapter 11

Can an Old Dog Change Its Spots?

Can an old dog learn new tricks? YES

Can a leopard change its spots? YES...but since it is a cat (one of the five "big cats" in the genus Panthera), it knows it doesn't have to entertain humans by doing so, and therefore we are stuck with the age-old dictum "A leopard cannot change its spots."

Can an old dog change its spots? YES... and will happily do so to please its humans.

After all, dogs patiently let us dress them up for Halloween and parties and parades and for no other reason than that it is Tuesday, or the anniversary of the day you learned to ride a bicycle without training wheels.

They let us teach them tricks such as balancing a biscuit on their snout and then tossing it in the air to catch. They let us shampoo, condition, fluff, trim, and put bows in their hair and then lead them out to a show ring or poke them into a designer handbag.

Dogs are very indulgent with us.

And therefore, dogs would willingly change their spots, their brindle stripes, or even reverse their white socks on black legs to black socks on white, if it would elicit a smile from their people.

Dogs understand it's all a matter of being <u>willing</u> to change, something that far too many humans just won't embrace.

My dog Sugar Bear validated this theory during the week I was writing this book. We've been going to Central Park every morning, since moving to NYC from Los Angeles two years ago. Other than rainy days, or her first winter where she hibernated for six months and refused to take walks at all, or if it's snowing heavily, we do go every morning. Some sloping areas have metal railings along the path to keep people off the grass and out from under low hanging tree branches, but the dogs jump over the rails, go between the rails, or scoot under the rails to run and play in those areas.

Whenever Sugar Bear would see a dog on the other side of the rail, she'd do the play bow, and they'd romp, but always separated by the railing. I encouraged her to go ahead and step over the middle rail but she didn't seem to understand what was needed on her part.

This went on month after month, and I accepted that she would simply never be a dog that tried to get on the other side of a fence. She never had, and why would she suddenly change her "spots" on this topic?

It seemed she would never "catch on" or understand how the other dogs managed to get over onto the grassy slopes where they romped and chased balls thrown by their owners from the concrete path.

And then it happened. This was just two days ago.

She saw a Golden dancing around on the other side of the rail, and she hopped that middle rail and began playing with him. Tears filled my eyes.

When the other dog ran off and leaped the fence to go further into the park, Sugar Bear stood forlornly, looking at me from the other side of the railing, flummoxed.

Together, we watched a little dog scoot under the lowest rail. She poked her head there, but pulled back: Nope, too small.

She saw two more dogs leap over the top, and stared: Nope, too tall.

Finally, while I waited with baited breath and alternately cheered her on (go ahead, try to hold your breath and cheer at the same time—you have to alternate) … she stepped over that middle rail to join me and then pranced down the path like she was queen of the walk.

Another dog owner was watching all this. I turned to her and said, "I feel as proud as if my two-year-old just learned to tie her shoes all by herself!"

She nodded, understanding completely.

Before we get to the all-important survey coming up in the next chapter about what Trump's voters were thinking when they picked him on Election Day, I want to take a moment to insert a few lessons on the topic of thinking. It's a process similar to sneaking broccoli into your kids' macaroni and cheese and hoping they won't realize you are doing something for their own good.

The rest of this chapter is therefore now called:

THOUGHT, DE-MYSTIFIED

Most of us were raised to believe that the ever-present stream of silent messages, images and random ideas passing through our mind is called "thinking." Wrong. That's primarily "mental activity" such as instant comments about what we observe and what others are doing around us, reactions to something we do or don't want in our lives, and so on.

Thought requires more work. That's why so few people bother with it. It's so much easier to go through life reacting to what others are doing, complaining about conditions, and finding someone else to blame when things go wrong.

But then along came quantum physics and gave us a peek into an entirely different way of looking at the universe and everything in it, including ourselves.

Out went the old idea that life happens to us, and we just have to do our best with the hand we were dealt (or as we said in my Catholic family, *We all have a cross to bear*).

That outside-in perspective of life meant everyone had to struggle and fight to try to get their share of food, money and everything else because there was a limited amount of anything you could name, even goodwill. Only a favored few enjoyed wealth, and the rest had to suffer in victimhood. That was what I call the Old Worldview.

But with a quantum-based understanding (still in its early stages, but so exciting—told ya I'm a nerd!) that we participate in our results by virtue of our thought vibrations, in came the New Worldview.

This is an abundant, benevolent universe that happily responds to our vibrational requests. But the law of attraction must MATCH the frequency of our desires so that if we get in harmony with DT we end up with DT. That's why it's so important not to hate or push against his policies.

We must work to change, by being positive and confident in our ability to manifest the desired end results.!

(May I confess something? I just typed about 10 exclamation points at the end of the sentence above, but I was afraid you'd think it was too much, so I deleted them. Well, maybe I'll go back and put just one, right after the period, so it looks like maybe just a teensy typo. Okay, thanks. That felt good.)

We do indeed create our reality, and when it is something on as large a scale as Trump's election, we must understand that no matter how much we'd like to point to Republicans and say "They did it!"… we Democrats and Progressives played an important part, too.

I explain this topic in greater detail in my book *America's New Breed of Freedom Fighters* which was published on Inauguration Day 2017.

Two of the challenges we liberals and progressives face are how to reach the non-voters to help them see the value of getting involved in the creation of our civilization so that American freedoms remain free and unsullied, and how to entice the moderate Republican voters to examine their beliefs and their thinking about issues such as free press, free speech, an economy that serves the nation, not just the super-wealthy, access to health care and education, protecting our environment for future generations, and so many more aspects of our complex modern lives.

Apathy of the non-voters combined with the Republicans' certainty of "My party, right or wrong!" reveal to us the prevalence of thought habits that would benefit from a higher level of awareness about life and all we can create when we step out of the role of victim.

However, if it were simply a matter of sharing information, we could print doorstep flyers or post in social media in known Republican hangouts.

We all know what happens when you try to convince someone to do what you want. That other person just digs in their heels and becomes even more insistent that you are wrong and they are right. It seems to be human nature that we don't want change that is thrust upon us—we want to be the ones deciding for ourselves what we wish to change. We want to choose what we believe in, even when our hidden beliefs would never stand up to examination in the light of day.

I was a very picky eater as a child, and I remember one time in particular when my mother asked me –begged me – to at least eat three peas she had carefully spooned on my plate, instead of simply telling her *I hate peas*. I can remember exactly where I was sitting, at her right hand. With my chin up, I looked at her coolly and said with all the logic of a nine-year-old, "But what if I taste them? And I like them? Then I would have to eat them. But I hate peas." I still don't eat peas. To me it's a preference, something I don't give thought to. It doesn't matter to anyone else whether I eat peas or not. Does it?

But it does matter to millions of people when voters with the power to move in the direction of progress, simply stick by their paradigm "I'm a Republican and that means I vote Republican" and blindly elect a man with a declared agenda of devastation and destruction and racism.

That's not thinking. It's mindlessly following an old idea inserted in the child's mind to vote Republican along with a post-hypnotic command to never question whether the candidate is right or wrong and deserves that vote.

Here is what Wikipedia has to say about "Thought": *Mental activity involving an individual's subjective consciousness. Thought refers to ideas or arrangements of ideas that are the result of the process of thinking. Though thinking is an activity considered essential to humanity, there is no general consensus as to how we define or understand it.*

Because thought underlies many human actions and interactions, understanding its physical and metaphysical origins, processes, and effects has been a longstanding goal of many academic disciplines including linguistics, psychology, neuroscience, philosophy, artificial intelligence, biology, sociology and cognitive science.

Thinking allows humans to make sense of, interpret, represent or model the world they experience, and to make predictions about that world. It is therefore helpful to an organism with needs, objectives, and desires as it makes plans or otherwise attempts to accomplish those goals.

***

Now you can see why random reactive messages in our minds are not really "thought." When you say to someone, "What are you thinking about?" you usually don't want to hear a verbatim stream of consciousness report. You want to know what is going on in his or her life, what they are up to, what issue they are contemplating or relationship they might be wishing to improve, or a trip they'd like to talk about.

Most of us grew up learning to report facts, because we were punished for daydreaming, but it turns out, in the light of quantum physics, that our daydreams and hidden desires are powerful tools of the mind. What we really believe we deserve and will receive determine our results and outcomes. That's why so many people are frustrated by positive affirmations, and say things like "the law of attraction is stupid—it doesn't work!"

More on the power of thought is included in my book America's New Breed of Freedom Fighters and also my book on the law of attraction called You Were Born to Triumph: Create a Five-Star Life in Your Quantum Kitchen

Let's do a quick overview, by diving into knowledge presented to the world on the topic of thinking by Thomas Troward, a renowned philosopher. His only student was the American woman Genevieve Behrend who manifested the money necessary to study with him at length in England by using the principles of attraction that he taught in essays and lectures she had already studied avidly.

Attaining Your Desires by Genevieve Behrend is set up in the manner of a student and teacher in dialogue, with "GB" indicating the student, Genevieve Behrend, and "Sage" meaning Thomas Troward himself. Because her summary of her private coaching from Toward is so condensed and valuable, I'm including several excerpts from different parts of her book, starting below:

What I wish particularly to convey to you within these pages is the method of scientific right thinking, and to awaken in you the desire to try to use this method in order to form the habit of thinking only the

thoughts you wish to see crystallized in a worthy achievement or result. In addition, I want to direct your thoughts toward a better understanding of that Spirit of God, or Good, which points the way to the roseate dawn of a new civilization.

***

The sages of the centuries, each one tincturing their thought with their own soul essence, have united in telling us that, "As a man thinketh in his heart, so is he." It has been established by the experience of the ages that always the law is the same. But how shall one think in their heart, so that only goodness may blossom and ripen into rich deed and rare result?"

***

Adverse circumstances are overcome by reversing the originating cause, which is your own thought. Anxiety and fear always attract conditions of their own kind. Reverse this tendency and entertain only those thoughts which register harmony and confident assurance, and the adverse circumstances will recede, and in their place will appear the conditions which correspond to your changed mentality.

***

GB: Now I would like to know if we inherit our tendencies of mind?

Sage: Most of us inherit our thoughts, just as we inherit the color of our eyes. If you intend to understand the relation existing between mental action and material conditions sufficiently well to control your circumstances, you must think for yourself, and in your own way, irrespective of what your ancestors thought, even though some of them might have brought desired results."

***

GB: *There are times when I become cross and impatient with myself because I give way to anxiety and fear (the very things which I know now will cause my defeat). And yet I will do it, just as I will eat something I like even though I know it will disagree with me. Could you give me a formula to use at such times?*

Sage: *When the triad of enemies --fear, anxiety, and discouragement -- assails you, poisoning your mind and body, weakening your power to attract what you want, begin instantly to take deep breaths, and repeat as fast as you can, aloud or silently, the following affirmation, which is an antidote to the poison and a powerful assurance and attraction of Good: "The Life in me is inseverably connected with all the life that exists, and it is entirely devoted to my personal advancement." If you are alert and can make this affirmative thought overlap the negative, anxious suggestion, you will very soon free yourself.*

***

Thank you, Genevieve and Thomas.

I think it's particularly important to realize that we inherit the bulk of our thinking from our parents and teachers, and the influence of people we admire and trust. Unlike the sitcom *Growing Pains*, life isn't always jolly if a member of your family is a staunch Republican in a house of liberals, or vice versa. We instinctively want to protect what we feel are our most

109

important values and beliefs.

In the first book in this series, America's New Breed of Freedom Fighters, I mentioned that I grew up in the southwest. My mother was a Republican. She was raised in Utah in an era when being a Republican meant you were voting for a smaller government at the federal level and more control at the state level. My dad was born and raised in Louisiana during a time when every good Southerner was a Democrat.

My mother remained a Republican until Nixon came along again as a presidential candidate, having been defeated years earlier by John F. Kennedy in 1960. She supported the ERA (Equal Rights Amendment). I don't know how many Republican women did that. The most vocal ones certainly did not and were angrily determined to keep women in their "proper" place in society.

The Republicans systematically stonewalled the ERA year after year; it never was approved.

It is particularly troubling to me how many Stepford wives a.k.a. Republican wives consistently support men like Donald Trump who trample the rights of women and wipe their feet on human rights in general.

Here's the question before us: *Can non-voters and Republicans change their spots?*

Chapter 12

Vulcan Mind-Meld with Trump's Voters

I attended Catholic school for 12 years and when we had a particularly challenging assignment, invariably one of the nuns would say, "Girls and boys, put your thinking caps on!"

I always wished that they had little hats in a box that they would pass around for all of us to wear. Of course, looking back now that I've been a parent, you don't want kids to get hair lice from sharing hats, so maybe it was just as well. However, in this survey of Trump's voters, I did borrow a friend's "brain hat," as you will learn below.

After conducting the first survey the day after the 2016 election to find out WHY Republicans voted for Donald Trump, I was still not satisfied with what I had learned. I tabulated the emotional reasons for their choice, but I wanted to know what they were actually THINKING when they selected a man so completely unqualified for the office.

I decided a second survey would be needed. However, since Donald Trump was already in office by then and slashing grants for scientific studies, and since the Democrats had already coughed up $1.5 billion for my first survey – Shout out to all Hillary supporters: *Thanks guys! Love ya! #Demforce* – I didn't feel it was right to ask for more donations.

Although I'm currently living in New York City to be closer to family, I lived in Los Angeles for most of my life. For many years I attended the annual "The Los Angeles Times Festival of Books," the largest book festival in the country, when it was held on the grounds of UCLA each spring.

A few years ago, while browsing the festival booths and mingling with thousands of book lovers, authors and publishers, I saw a golf cart go by, headed for one of the buildings where famous authors would be speaking at scheduled times. You needed a ticket in advance for those events, and I had come to the fair at the last minute, so the sold-out notices were my draw of the day.

As the golf cart turned, I noticed that on the back bench seat, facing outwards, Leonard Nimoy was riding. I watched for a moment, silently thanking him for all the years of being Mr. Spock.

I assumed he was heading to speak to an audience and would then be autographing copies of his books. His autobiography was in two volumes. The first, written in 1975, was called *I Am Not Spock*. Well, all his fans knew that was just a blind to keep his cover, and sure enough, he came out with volume two twenty years later, admitting *I Am Spock*.

While thinking about the kind of survey I could do with a zero budget and 60-odd million people to reach, I thought about time travel, and what I would have done at the Book Festival that day when I saw Leonard Nimoy, if only I could have seen into the future and learned about Donald Trump in time to discuss our current dilemma with Spock.

Even just a few years ago, at the time of that book fair, Trump was simply a smug, smirking guy you heard bragging about money or blasting people and groping women on a TV reality show. A total narcissist. I couldn't watch his show because I cringe every time he opens his mouth.

So... using the incredible power of "What if...?" let's return to that Book Festival and tweak the ending. Instead of silently letting the golf cart drive away from me...

I saw Nimoy's golf cart stop to let pedestrians pass. There was room on the seat next to him. I sped to the cart, smiling.

Me: May I join you a moment?

Apparently, I looked harmless (I get that reaction all the time), because he indicated the seat beside him and I hopped on. The golf cart jerked forward. I knew our time together would be limited due to the speaker's schedule, so I got to the point quickly.

Me: I'm a fan, I'm a writer, but I'm also a dreamer. I had a prophetic dream about you and about America. I was looking into the future in early 2017, a time when you will be greatly needed but you will have died two years earlier.

He was intrigued but frowning at the same time.

Me: Oh, sorry, I guess I shouldn't have mentioned you're going to die in February of 2015.

He shrugged philosophically, but remained silent.

As I explained about Donald Trump, his frown grew more intense.

Me: Mr. Spock, we'll need you desperately but you won't be there to help us! You'll be on Vulcan by then.

He nodded, not surprised by my comment. Finally, he spoke.

Nimoy: It is home.

The golf cart driver pulled up in front of a red brick building where a sign announced that Leonard Nimoy would be speaking at 3:00. It was nearly that already, but I had more to say, more to accomplish in this very special visit with him.

We got off the cart, Spock thanked the driver, and we walked slowly towards a side door in the building, away from the queue awaiting him.

Nimoy: I know what you want to ask of me.

Me: I know you know. I wouldn't expect anything less, sir. Will you show me how to do it?

Nimoy: The good of the many outweighs the needs of the one.

Me: I knew you would understand. Um, I'm sorry I told you about when you are going to Vulcan. That was tactless.

Nimoy: We are eternal beings. I never expected to inhabit this body forever. Live long and prosper, my new friend. Now let us find a quiet corner and I will teach you what you want to know.

And so, that is how I learned how to do the Vulcan Mind Meld.

Please do not write and ask me to teach you, because I promised I would not divulge the technique to anyone. Even Bill Shatner.

I wish now that I had also asked Spock to show me how to do the Vulcan nerve pinch, because it surely is needed on Capitol Hill more and more every day that Trump remains in office and his cronies continue to spread devastation everywhere.

After leaving Leonard Nimoy, I had my answer: my second survey would be conducted via a massive Vulcan Mind Meld with 60-odd million Republicans.

By the time I returned from my spin through time, my Skype line was buzzing. It was Bill Shatner.

Bill: Hey, Evelyn!

Me [startled]: You know my name?

Bill: I've been reading some of your books. Why didn't you tell me you're not Elaine?

Not waiting for my answer, he began laughing, his eyes twinkling mischievously.

Bill: So I hear you've been time traveling and met up with Nimoy. I bet he made you promise not to show me how to do that little trick of his.

Me: Um, yes. Sorry.

Bill: I was at the other end of it more than once. Never really cared about doing it myself. But are you sure you should go through with this? No one's ever done a Mind Meld on such a large scale, not even on Vulcan. 60 million minds assaulting you all at once could be quite a dangerous mission. Not one I'd send an Away Team on, not without protection.

Me: But I've created a shield, so I think I'll be okay.

Bill: Let me see it.

Me: It's not something you can see. I'm a wordsmith so I made it out of words.

Bill: Tell me, then.

Me: Okay, it goes like this: "I am a blessed child of the

Universe and I now invoke the protection of all who love and care for me. Only people who are harmonious and kind, and who intend benevolence toward me will be allowed to connect with my mind, and the connection will instantly dissolve at the first sign of discord."

Bill: Hey, I like that. When are you doing the Mind Meld?

Me: Tonight, because I want to put the results in my new book and it comes out on Presidents Day.

Bill: Are those coordinates you gave me last time still the same? That's why I called.

Me: Yes...

Even as I spoke, I noticed the familiar shimmer and glimmer of an object being transported to my desk. It wasn't big enough to be the Universal Translator again.

It finished materializing. I gasped in surprise and looked back at the screen where Kirk was grinning knowingly.

I couldn't find words, not a comfortable position for a writer to be in: *speechless*.

He seemed to know what I was thinking as I pinned on the Comm Badge he'd sent me.

Bill: I'll be on hand if you need me. Kirk out.

After that, the only thing for me to do was put on the brain hat which a friend of mine loaned me, and set about conducting my Mind Meld survey with Trump's voters.

Oh, what's a brain hat? It's exactly what it sounds like, a hat knit to look like a brain, complete with ridges and grayness and bumps. The doggy Mom of Sugar Bear's friend Lily, a miniature Italian greyhound we see at Central Park now and then, had told me she was knitting a "brain hat" for the Science March in NYC. She is a working scientist, and after hearing about the march, I signed up to volunteer in support of their group. She was thrilled to know that I'd be wearing her hat during the Mind Meld.

The only problem is that the Science March isn't for another two months, so she wasn't finished knitting the hat. No worries. We put little rubber bumpers on the ends of the knitting needles so they wouldn't poke me in the head, and tucked the trailing ends of yarn underneath. She offered to take a photo I could include in the book, but I respectfully declined and went home. I did get a few looks on Park Avenue, but you could wear just about anything on the streets of Manhattan and get away with it, so a brain hat was no big deal.

I got home and found that I kept glancing at the clock, waiting for the optimal time which Spock had helped me to calculate.

Finally, it was time to start the survey. I felt a little nervous, so I asked Sugar Bear to sit on the couch next to me and lend me her calming energy.

I made sure the brain hat was firmly in place.

Then I put up my protective shield.

I tapped the Comm Badge.

Bill: Kirk here.

Me: I'm starting now.

Bill: You don't have to do this—

Me: Yes, I do. I want to find out how this happened, how Trump got elected. I want to find out and then tell everyone what those voters were thinking.

Bill: Stay in touch.

Me: I will.

I signed off.

My hands were jittery, so I took a few deep breaths and mentally began the process that Spock had taught me.

I knew I needed to remain relaxed and confident, but I kept bracing myself for what might come next.

Take a moment to imagine the position I was putting myself in: opening my mind to connect with 60-odd million people who had selected Donald Trump as the best choice to lead our beautiful country as its President.

Sugar Bear sensed my fright, and snuggled closer.

I continued with the process.

I had told Spock I wanted to send out an initial question, whose answer would then trigger the one question in the survey itself.

So I posed the preliminary question to my target audience: *This survey is only for people who actually voted for Donald Trump. Do you admit that you voted for Donald Trump to be elected President of the United States? Please respond "yes" or "no" in your mind right now.*

All 60-odd million replied "Yes," so I took another deep breath and transmitted the questionnaire:

Please share what you were thinking on Election Day when you cast your vote for Donald Trump.

Embedded in the question were instructions to use your own words, and omit quoting Trump's campaign promises, Trump's tweets, Trump's soundbites on Fox News, and to share only what you were THINKING when you chose him.

I sat for a long time.

I transmitted the survey again, thinking perhaps I hadn't reached anyone.

Spock had shown me how to bypass the limitations of time zones, so I knew that bedtime wasn't creating any barriers.

Still no response. But I was getting the pings back, tallied on a counter Spock had slipped into my hand before we parted. The counter worked fine in the preliminary question, and now I could see the numbers mounting up as voter after voter acknowledged receipt of the survey question itself... Voter #1.... 149,567, 678,092, 4,973,104...29,877,023...

There were no responses. Voter after voter... Nothing... Getting thirsty... Maybe I should give up on finding out what Trump's voters were thinking...

WAIT, here comes a reply!

Trump Voter #49,999,999

What was I thinking? ... Well, I guess I was thinking about how on earth I'd explain to my parents and everybody at work and all my neighbors if I didn't vote the Republican ticket and ... I was also thinking that I was still pretty sure all those awful things I heard about Trump weren't true. So I voted for him. But ... now I see he's the one who lied. First day in office and the Civil Rights and Marriage Equality tabs vanish from the White House official web site? That's not right. He shouldn't be allowed to do stuff like that. This is America, not Russia or someplace like that. I go to Planned Parenthood for cancer screenings. This isn't what I thought would happen. I thought it meant factory jobs and a better economy—that's what I was thinking. But... Please—tell me—how can I help now? What can I do? I'm so sorry...

Trump Voter #50,000,000 What were you THINKING? Please use your own words....

No response...

Trump Voter #60,000,666 What were you THINKING? Please use your own words....

No response...

I finally sat back, pulled off the brain hat and carefully set it aside so my friend could finish knitting it for the Science March in NYC on Earth Day.

I tapped my Comm Badge.

Bill: How did it go?

Me: Pretty much what I expected. They weren't thinking at all. They were just reacting.

Chapter 13

GSDs for DT's WMDs

The other day, while walking in Central Park with Sugar Bear, I heard two women behind me chatting about their jobs as they straggled along with their own dogs.

And then one of them said, "Oh, look at that gorgeous German shepherd!"

My head swiveled. *Where? Where?* I had an instant picture in my mind: He'd be wearing *lederhosen* (because otherwise how had they realized he was German?) and of course he had to be holding a shepherd's staff and perhaps herding a lamb or two through the park.

New York City has parades just about every other weekend for every holiday, group and organization you can imagine, so I thought there might be some festival or parade I hadn't heard about.

I didn't see anyone who looked even close to knowing what *lederhosen* look like, let alone wear the outfit. All the guys were ambling along in jeans and sweats and hooded jackets, or running in skintight Lycra, with nary a shepherd's staff or crook in sight.

And then a big tan and black dog ran past me. I realized the women had meant "German Shepherd Dog" not "German shepherd." A GSD is a dog. A German shepherd is a German guy/gal who works on a sheep farm. Now you know.

We could use a few GSDs in DC.

That's Washington, D.C., of course.

They could keep an eye on DT and his wolves, and help protect the flock. (I know you know who I mean by "DT," right?)

While we're on the acronyms list, let's look at WMDs: Weapons of Mass Destruction.

Words can be weapons, especially when the person wielding the words has the power to create executive orders that destroy freedom in one swipe of the pen.

WMDs: Weapons of attitude. *Hey, I've got the rights that I need, so who cares if you've got yours?*

WMDs: Weapons of annoyance: *I wish those protestors would just get over it. They're making such a big fuss over nothing.*

WMDs: Weapons of medieval thinking: *I don't believe in climate change. Therefore, I will refuse to listen to anything related to it. End of subject.*

I have yet to hear a marcher say that they only want Planned Parenthood centers to stay open for women who bring proof they voted for Hillary.

I have yet to hear a Democratic senator or congressperson say, "We will keep moving forward for clean air, health care, education, and so on. But all Republican children must be removed from the public school system and refused access to public libraries. All Republican women must go back to the days when employers could refuse to hire single women if they admitted on an application that they hoped to get married one day. All Republicans must accept less than minimum wage from employers like Trump and his cronies, even when we manage to pass a bill raising the minimum wage to a more livable amount. And all Republicans of color who voted for Trump—get to the back of the bus."

My dad was a U.S. Army Colonel, Retired. In World War Two, he was in the OSS, which later became the CIA. Growing up, I never lived on an army base, but the military influence was evident in my family's household.

Sometimes my older sisters and I would hear him call out from the living room: *Front and center!* and we knew to stop what we were doing and go see what he wanted. Sometimes Ed Sullivan had a special guest on that he thought we'd enjoy, like Topo Gigio, an adorable mouse puppet, or a troop of Chinese acrobats, or those guys who spin saucers on top of a narrow stick.

When I was in high school, my dad would snap on the overhead bedroom light promptly at 6:00 am on school days and announce, *Rise and shine!*

Unquestioning obedience has always been drilled into the military. It's a vital part of the discipline required for troops to fall in and move without standing around discussing what to do next, like you're planning the neighborhood barbecue and deciding who should bring what. *Okay, people with their last name beginning A to F, you bring salads...*

But when that habit of blind obedience to orders bleeds into civilian life, it's easy to see from the perspective of an observer that issues which should be questioned and should be discussed and should be disobeyed are instead saluted.

I know a lot of Republicans are military. It's a tradition. But I think it's one tradition (on a long list) that needs to be revisited by thinking soldiers and their families.

Democrats promote and vote for veteran rights, for benefits for military families. Republicans are always too busy looking at the bottom line and cutting budgets. I know that's what Republicans mean about a "smaller" federal government, but there's got to be a compromise so the citizens of our country get the benefits and support they need, instead of the DT focus on increasing profits for overgorged super-wealthy executives. (Yes, I know overgorged is one of those compound words that is redundant, like saying "hot water heater," but it fits the situation, doesn't it?)

Dear Republicans, Can you really not see that you vote against your own interests when you align your voting power with men like Donald Trump?

I wish my parents were still alive so I could ask their opinion about all that's going on right now in our great country.

But wishes aren't horses. We can't give a tug on the reins to turn around and sit down and say, "And by the way, tell me about the war, Daddy."

Tell me what it was like to be a newlywed with a baby (my oldest sister) and suddenly the whole world changed on December 7, 1941. He was based in Burma, so my mother moved while pregnant to Sacramento, California where both my oldest sisters were born. The family joke was always to try to figure out the logic of the War Office in sending a man who was born and raised in Louisiana and was fluent in English and French out to Asia where he knew not one word of the local language. Why didn't the Army send him to France? We'll never know.

But I would say to him today, given the chance, "Tell me about being in the OSS and about the Allies and the evil you defeated. Tell me what people were thinking and doing to keep their spirits up in the face of hate and destruction. Tell me. I promise I'll listen this time— instead of rolling my eyes and acting bored that you dared to tell me about your life experiences when I wanted to listen to the Beatles."

On 12/8/1941, President Franklin D. Roosevelt announced: "Yesterday, December 7, 1941—a date which will live in infamy—the United States of America was suddenly and deliberately attacked by naval and air forces of the Empire of Japan."

For us, now, at this point on the pages of history, the day that will long live in infamy is November 9, 2016.

Chapter 14

The Company You Keep

Remember in high school when you started hanging out with someone your parents didn't approve of? And they warned you about being around other teens who would be a bad influence, that it was too easy to slip into behavior not congruent with who you really were?

They said that if everyone else was doing it and you didn't want to be teased for not going along with the crowd, you'd end up being tarred with the same brush as them.

Turns out our parents were right, weren't they? If you hang out with the kids who have a bad reputation, you end up with one yourself even if you don't actually do all the stuff they're doing. People assumed you were just like them, warts and all, or why else would you be going around with them?

It's true now with Republicans. If you secretly don't like what Donald Trump is doing, then step away from your party! Create a brand new party if you want to keep the elements of a conservative platform that make sense to you.

But when you hang out with a racist like Trump, a misogynist and abuser like Trump, well, what on earth are we supposed to think about YOU?

From my knowledge of political history, it appears that the Republican Party began marching to a different drummer under Nixon's leadership.

Today, the cadence of Trump's drill team is that of jackboots and stiff arm salutes to a corrupt businessman.

And yet, Republicans voted for him anyway.

Maybe we should gather a convention of regression-hypnotists and find out where all that Nazi energy from the end of World War Two went.

Were Republicans hypnotized by Trump's rant? "Hate! Hate! Hate! Make America great!"

Were they blind to the truth of his corruption and total lack of experience and qualifications to be president because they refused to look past Fox News soundbites, Trump's tweets, and his hate messages about the Democratic platform and Hillary?

Or do Republicans as a whole actually agree that a "great" America is one that rolls back to when white settlers arrived from Europe and began slaughtering the "Redskins" living from sea to sea and mountain to desert?

As time moved along, and the land was cleared by destroying

Native Americans *en masse*, a new nation was conceived with liberty and justice for free white men (indentured servants didn't get a vote even if they were white males).

Somehow, inexplicably to me, a skewed nostalgia for the 1950s is driving the Republican Party today.

I don't think that all Republicans "should" become Democrats. But I do believe it would be of great value to our nation if those who continue to call themselves Republican even in the face of Trump's animosity and corruption would take time to look a whole lot closer at the responsibility that goes with the right to vote.

And if you don't align with Trump's values, why are you still supporting him? Why are you looking the other way and tutting at protestors?

Why not investigate the issues and then join us? We won't shame you for the choices you've made up until now. We'll make you welcome.

Consider this your invitation. #StandIndivisible

Chapter 15

Movie Quotes for Freedom Fighters

AMERICA, THE MELTING POT

Clueless

Cher (Alicia Silverstone): So like, right now for example. The Haitians need to come to America. But some people are all, "What about the strain on our resources?" Well it's like when I had this garden party for my father's birthday, right? I put R.S.V.P. 'cause it was a sit-down dinner. But some people came that like did not R.S.V.P. I was like totally buggin'. I had to haul ass to the kitchen, redistribute the food, and squish in extra place settings. But by the end of the day it was, like, the more the merrier. And so if the government could just get to the kitchen, rearrange some things, we could certainly party with the Haitians. And in conclusion may I please remind you it does not say R.S.V.P. on the Statue of Liberty. Thank you very much.

from *Clueless* (1995) written by Amy Heckerling, inspired by Jane Austen's *Emma*

Home Alone

Kevin McCallister (Macaulay Culkin): This is my house, I have to defend it.

from *Home Alone* (1990) written by John Hughes

Finding Neverland

J.M. Barrie (Johnny Depp): You find a glimmer of happiness in this world, there's always someone who wants to destroy it.

from *Finding Neverland* (2004) written by David Magee, based on the play by Allan Knee

Fences

Bono (Stephen Henderson): Some people build fences to keep people out, and other people build fences to keep people in.

from *Fences* (2016) by August Wilson

Groundhog Day

Phil (Bill Murray): I'm not going to live by their rules anymore.

from *Groundhog Day* (1993) written by Danny Rubin and Harold Ramis

THE BROTHERHOOD OF MAN

Avatar

Jake Sully (Sam Worthington): I see you.

Neytiri (Zoë Saldana): I see you.

from *Avatar* (2009) written by James Cameron

Stardust

Yvaine (Claire Danes): The little I know about love is that it's unconditional. It's not something you can buy.

from *Stardust* (2007) written by Jane Goldman & Matthew Vaughn, based on the novel by Neil Gaiman

UNITED WE STAND

Shrek the Musical

Shrek, Fiona, Donkey and the Fairy Tale Characters (singing):

What makes us special makes us strong…

We are different and united

We are us and we are you

This is our story, this is our story

This is our story!

God bless us, everyone

from *Shrek the Musical* (2013) by William Steig and David Lindsay-Abaire

A RIP IN THE FORCE FIELD

Star Wars (the original)

Obi-Wan (Alec Guinness): I felt a great disturbance in the Force, as if millions of voices suddenly cried out in terror and were suddenly silenced. I fear something terrible has happened.

from *Star Wars* (later renamed *Star Wars: Episode IV – A New Hope*) (1977) written by George Lucas

THE POWER OF PERSISTENCE

Finding Nemo

Dory (voice by Ellen DeGeneres): Just keep swimming!

from *Finding Nemo* (2003) written by Andrew Stanton

The Dish

Cliff Buxton (Sam Neill): My wife said something. She said, "Failure is never quite so frightening as regret."

Glenn Latham (Tom Long): Oh, that's good advice.

from *The Dish* (2000) written by Santo Cilauro & Tom Gleisner & Jane Kennedy & Rob Sitch

12 Years a Slave

Solomon Northup (Chiwetel Ejiofor): I will not fall into despair! I will keep myself hardy until freedom is opportune!

from *12 Years a Slave* (2013) written by John Ridley, based on Solomon Northup's autobiography

TIME IS OF THE ESSENCE

The Imitation Game

Alan Turing (Benedict Cumberbatch): Some people thought we were at war with the Germans. Incorrect. We were at war with the clock.

from *The Imitation Game* (2014) written by Graham Moore

LIVING AT OUR HIGHEST POTENTIAL

Amélie

Narrator (André Dussollier): Amelie has a strange feeling of absolute harmony. It's a perfect moment. A soft light, a scent in the air, the quiet murmur of the city. A surge of love, an urge to help mankind overcomes her.

from *Amélie (Le Fabuleux Destin d'Amélie Poulain)* (2001) written by Guillaume Laurant and Jean-Pierre Jeunet

Like Stars on Earth

Ram Shankar Nikumbh (Aamir Khan): There have been such

gems amongst us, who changed the course of the world, because they could look at the world differently. Their thinking was unique and not everyone understood them. They were opposed, yet they emerged winners and the world was amazed.

from *Like Stars on Earth (Taare Zameen Par)* (2007) written by Amole Gupte

<u>WHO & WHAT WE ARE UP AGAINST</u>

The Sound of Music

Max (Richard Haydn): What's going to happen's going to happen. Just make sure it doesn't happen to you.

Captain von Trapp (Christopher Plummer): Max. Don't you <u>ever</u> say that again.

Max: You know I have no political convictions. Can I help it if other people do?

Captain von Trapp: Oh yes, you can help it. You must help it.

from *The Sound of Music* (1965) written by Ernest Lehman (screenplay)

Love Actually

[Speaking to the British Prime Minister (Hugh Grant)]

The U.S. President (Billy Bob Thornton): I'll give you

138

anything you ask for, as long as it's not something I don't wanna give.

from *Love Actually* (2003) written by Richard Curtis

Gone with the Wind

Rhett Butler (Glark Gable) [AS IF TO DONALD TRUMP]: You're like the thief who isn't the least bit sorry he stole, but is terribly, terribly sorry he's going to jail.

from *Gone with the Wind* (1939) written by Sydney Howard, based on the novel by Margaret Mitchell

Life Is Beautiful

Guido (Roberto Benigni): What are your political views?

Other Man: [speaking to his two sons] Benito, Adolf! Sit down! Sorry, Guido, what did you say?

from *Life Is Beautiful (La Vita è Bella)* (1997) written by Vincenzo Cerami and Roberto Benigni

Casablanca

Rick (Humphrey Bogart): I don't like disturbances in my place.

[to ~~the German officer~~ DONALD TRUMP]

Rick: Either lay off politics, or get out.

from *Casablanca* (1942) written by Julius J. Epstein and Philip

G. Epstein and Howard Koch, based on the play by Murray Burnett and Joan Alison

The Shawshank Redemption

Andy Dufresne (Tim Robbins): It's my life. Don't you understand? IT'S MY LIFE!

from *The Shawshank Redemption* (1994) written by Frank Darabont, from a short story by Stephen King

The Iron Lady

Margaret Thatcher (Meryl Streep): Watch your thoughts, for they become words. Watch your words, for they become actions. Watch your actions, for they become habits. Watch your habits, for they become your character. And watch your character, for it becomes your destiny. What we think, we become. My father always said that. And I think I am fine.

from *The Iron Lady* (2011) written by Abi Morgan

Life of Pi

Writer (Rafe Spall): So your story does have a happy ending.

Adult Pi Patel (Irrfan Khan): Well, that's up to you. The story's yours now.

from *Life of Pi* (2012) written by David Magee, based on the novel by Yann Martel

Chapter 16

Erma's Missing Socks

Erma Bombeck wrote over 4,000 syndicated newspaper columns. While writing this book, to keep my own spirits up while trying to say all I wanted to say but do so within a benevolent cloud of humor, I read *Forever, Erma: Best-Loved Writing from America's Favorite Humorist,* an anthology of her humorous essays about life in suburbia starting with her first column on September 4, 1965, and highlighting the years until her final column dated April 17, 1996, shortly before her death from cancer.

My mother was a big fan of Erma's and I grew up reading Erma's many other books. The anthology mentioned above is a great place to start if you are unfamiliar with her writing.

One of the recurring topics Erma touched on now and then was the perpetual mystery of how you can put six pairs of socks in the washer – or two pairs or twenty – and yet when you take out those socks, their mates have vanished.

Where did the vagrant socks go? They couldn't all have been swept down the drain with the dirty water. Otherwise, why didn't even smaller items go that route?

Her insightful way of addressing everyday issues we could all identify with, her steadfast efforts to get the Equal Rights Amendment passed, and her unflagging compassion for her readers inspired me throughout the writing of this book.

Erma knew she was dying. She'd been on the waiting list for a new kidney, but had refused to use her fame to jump to the top of the list. She passed away a few days after her last column appeared in print.

This quote is from that final newspaper column: "My deeds will be measured not by my youthful appearance, but by the concern lines on my forehead, the laugh lines around my mouth, and the chins from seeing what can be done for those smaller than me or who have fallen."

Erma once said, "When I stand before God at the end of my life, I would hope that I would not have a single bit of talent left, and could say, 'I used everything you gave me'."

That's my wish, too. And I hope it is yours.

In this time of great challenge with Trump's Administration and their powerful agenda of divisiveness, it is up to us, We the Progressives – to keep pushing forward with positive change to defend and promote liberty and justice for all.

Now, on behalf of Erma, I am sending out a message to all those missing socks, in the tradition of old-time telegrams that popularized this plea: *All is forgiven. Stop. Please come home. Stop.*

I'll let you know what (or who) shows up.

And when it comes time for me to go Home, I'll simply tap my Comm Badge and say, "One to beam up. Evelyn out."

About the Author

Evelyn with Sugar Bear
Photo by Ruth Wishengrad

Evelyn Roberts Brooks is a writer, lightworker, and speaker. She's shared the stage with Bob Proctor ("The Secret"), Gay Hendricks, Peggy McColl, Arielle Ford, Misa Hopkins, Dr. Steve G. Jones, and other experts in personal growth and development.

She's the author of over 20 fiction and non-fiction books including "AMERICA'S NEW BREED OF FREEDOM FIGHTERS;" "YOU WERE BORN TO TRIUMPH:

Create a Five-Star Life in Your Quantum Kitchen" as well as the Born to Triumph series of personal development books on individual topics; "FORGET YOUR TROUBLES: Enjoy Your Life Today;" "CALLING ALL LIGHTWORKERS;" "HEAL TOXIC FRIENDSHIPS" and other self-help books, as well as novels, including "THE DREAM SPINNERS." She's an optioned screenwriter (with a focus on family comedy and romantic comedy) and Nicholl Fellowship quarterfinalist.

She's also the founder of RestoringTibet.com Her book Restoring Tibet: Global Action Plan to Send the Dalai Lama Home debuted as the #1 bestseller in the category of War & Peace.

Evelyn is passionate about helping others experience a transformational healing in their lives, reduce stress, heal heartache from loss, divorce, grief and trauma, and lead happier lives.

With an emphasis on helping others gain clarity about the life changes they would like to make and then showing them how to expand in awareness, Evelyn inspires and encourages while making the lessons entertaining and inspiring.

Her goal is to help millions of people heal and be happier.

evelynbrooks.com

Read all the books in this series...

<u>Liberty and Justice Series</u>

by Evelyn Roberts Brooks

AMERICA'S NEW BREED OF FREEDOM FIGHTERS: With Liberty and Justice for All

WHAT WERE THEY THINKING?: Inside the Minds of Trump's Voters [Political humor]

WHAT TRUMP'S VOTERS WERE REALLY THINKING: The Complete Report Unedited [Political humor]

WHEN THEY GO LOW WE GO HIGH: Tending Our Garden of Democracy

CPSIA information can be obtained
at www.ICGtesting.com
Printed in the USA
FSHW020916161218
54513FS

9 781732 208018